D0436261

More Praise for Barbara Mahany

"Motherprayer is not just a book for mothers. It's a book, finally, about loving, and if you let it, it will transfigure how you see yourself as a giver and recipient of love."
—Lauren F. Winner, author of *Wearing God*

"In this fresh and richly lyrical work, Mahany takes us on a joy ride through the four seasons. Her poetic prose quickens our pulses and sends us on our way rejoicing."
—*Spirituality & Practice*

"A naturally heartfelt collection. Mahany has created an engaging, interactive work that does more than invite readers to participate in her observations of the Sacred—it compels her audience to seek out their own experiences. This woman is the real deal, reaching out to the wounded world with enlightened care and compassion."
—*Huffington Post*

"Always writing beautifully as a columnist for *The Chicago Tribune*, Mahany at last has a book, this one a series of essays, organized by seasons. The main dish is her writing, and she's stirred together fine words about simple things, frequently her children or life in an interfaith household (she is Christian, her husband Jewish). As a trained observer from years in journalism, Mahany is attentive to the smallest things. What's unique about the book—Mahany's singular voice. Those who open the pages are in for a literary treat, and the recipes are a lagniappe." —*Publishers Weekly*

"Balm for the hurried heart." —*Publishers Weekly*, picked *Slowing Time* "Top 10 Fall Best: Religion."

"This is truly an original work, offering litanies and prayers, poems and observations, essays and recipes, reflection ideas and action steps, all nicely arranged by the season of the year. This really is a book one can live with through a year. Mahany is a devout Catholic, a very good writer, with a large capacity, it seems, to see stuff; to attend. Rabbi Evan Moffic says she 'writes with the eyes of a sculptor and the ear of a poet.' Mahany has been a writer for *The Chicago Tribune*; this shows her journalistic chops quite nicely." —Hearts & Minds Books, "10 Great New Books Briefly Explained"

"*Slowing Time* is a very practical guide to learning how to slow down and be attentive to the abundant gifts of God that surround us at any given moment. By probing deeply the nooks and crannies of the home front, Mahany points out that the reader need not venture far to find what matters most. And the questions stirred will linger, long after the page is turned." —Relevant Magazine, "10 Books to Read this Fall for a Deeper Faith"

"*Publishers Weekly* named *Slowing Time* one of the 10 most anticipated religion books for the fall. But former *Chicago Tribune* reporter Barbara Mahany would like to tweak that: 'It's a spirituality book,' she said. 'I'm not a theologian. It's a book about paying attention.' A book for all seasons, *Slowing Time* unfurls month by month. Over three decades, Mahany put her inimitable stamp on human-interest stories. One of the most memorable was her characteristically compassionate 2004 profile of 'the Pigeon Man of Lincoln Square.' Mahany's heartbreaking farewell is included." — *Chicago Tribune*

"*Slowing Time* is at once a quiet feast for the soul and an eloquent response to a culture that's become obsessed with speed. With a poet's eye for detail and the quiet assurance of a born teacher, Barbara Mahany offers lessons gleaned from seasons of profound reflection and mindful observation—a manual of sorts for anyone who yearns to do less, feel more, engage with life at a deeper level, and see the world anew through eyes refreshed by wonder. And, really, isn't that each one of us? Read this lovely book and feel your own self soften, your heartbeat slow, your load lighten." —Katrina Kenison, author of *The Gift of an Ordinary Day* and *Magical Journey: An Apprenticeship in Contentment*

"This book is an original and a treasure. Mahany uses so many varied portals: fine-grained observations of the lovely and the hidden in nature, tiny astronomy lessons, an illuminating season-by-season calendar of holy days, and recipes (I liked 'Christmas-Eve Elves' French Toast) to guide the reader in the endangered art of slowing down enough to catch the sacred." —Dr. Wendy Mogel is a clinical psychologist and the author of *The Blessing of a Skinned Knee* and *The Blessing of a B Minus*

"In our hyper-e-networked world, too many of us live under the tyranny of the urgent. With *Slowing Time*, Barbara Mahany reminds us how not to lose sight of the things which are truly important—the beauty, serenity, and sanity that we can find in life's calm and quiet moments. Whether the chirping of a bird, the tingle of an autumn breeze, or the hug of a child, Mahany helps us see that when we entertain the seemingly mundane dimensions of life, we are embracing the sacred!" —Jonathan L. Walton; Plummer Professor of Christian Morals and Pusey Minister in the Memorial Church, Harvard University

"Barbara Mahany writes with the eyes of a sculptor and the ear of a poet. Her words remind us of what communities of faith do best—give us the tools and perspective to see the beauty around us and find ways to bring that beauty into everything we do." —Rabbi Evan Moffic, Congregation Solel, Highland Park, IL; author and blogger *Huffington Post, Beliefnet*

"We need whatever we can get to help us pay closer attention, be more awake to the moment, more alive amidst the clamoring distractions of the internet age. Barbara Mahany gives us a treasure—a thorough, practical guide full of wisdom, blessings, recipes, luminous facts, and elegant language. With her as our astute and patient leader, we gain an intimate knowledge of the seasons." —Debbie Blue, founding minister House of Mercy, St. Paul, MN; author *Consider the Birds: A Provocative Guide to Birds of the Bible*

"This is a book for those longing to find their way into the holy depths of life— precisely in the ordinary things close at hand. It is one long and exquisite hymn to life by a believer in the promise that beauty always happens for those 'with eyes to see.' *Slowing Time* invites us into that precious sanctuary of wonder in the very midst of our hurried and worried lives, refusing—with the sages and prophets through the ages—to separate the sacred from the profane. It is a book that breathes of spirit, dancing the first movements of hope into this often burdened and heavily laden world. It is a primer of the attentive heart, at once creative and practical and wise. In a world devoted to speed and managed efficiency, *Slowing Time* offers up the kind of poetic insight that might finally save us, page by page, moment by moment, season by season. If you are searching for that one book to deepen your soul and gentle your life and widen your heart, look no further." —Mark Burrows, poet, translator of *Prayers of a Young Poet: Rainer Maria Rilke*

BARBARA MAHANY

Motherprayer

LESSONS IN LOVING

Abingdon Press
Nashville

MOTHERPRAYER
LESSONS IN LOVING

Copyright © 2017 by Barbara Mahany

Library of Congress Cataloging-in-Publication Data has been requested.

ISBN 978-1-5018-2727-3

"Welcome Home, College Freshman. XOXO" by Barbara Mahany. Reprinted with permission of the *Chicago Tribune*; copyright *Chicago Tribune*; all rights reserved.

Excerpts reprinted with the permission of Fireside, a division of Simon & Schuster, Inc. from *Birder's Handbook* by Paul R. Ehrlich, David S. Dobkin, and Darryl Wheye. Copyright © 1988 by Paul R. Ehrlich, David S. Dobkin, Derryl. All rights reserved.

THE BIRDWATCHER'S HANDBOOK: A GUIDE TO THE NATURAL HISTORY OF THE BIRDS OF BRITAIN AND EUROPE edited by Paul R. Ehrlich, David S. Dobkin, and Darryl Wheye (1994): 287 words from pp. 369-371, 547, 235, 61, and 307. By permission of Oxford University Press.

Excerpts from *Laura's Birding Blog* reprinted with the permission of Laura Erickson.

17 18 19 20 21 22 23 24 25—10 9 8 7 6 5 4 3 2 1
MANUFACTURED IN THE UNITED STATES OF AMERICA

To Will, with whom it all begins,
To Teddy, with whom it begins again,
To Blair, who began it all,
To every blessed mother and motherfriend who has put flight to my
every hope and dream and whispered prayer,
You have birthed the holiest depths of me, each one of you.

I would like to beg you . . . as well as I can, to have patience with everything unresolved in your heart and to try to love the questions themselves *as if they were locked rooms or books written in a very foreign language. Don't search for the answers, which could not be given to you now, because you would not be able to live them. And the point is, to live everything.* Live *the questions now. Perhaps then, someday far in the future, you will gradually, without even noticing it, live your way into the answer.*

—Rainer Maria Rilke
Letters to a Young Poet[1]

Contents

Hatchling: Tender Soul Awakening 51

Brooding: Keeping Close Watch, Savoring All the While 77

Tending the Clutch: The Healing Balms of Motherhood 101

Nestling: At the Edge of the Nest 123

Fledgling: Taking Flight 143

Almost Empty Nest 163

And in the End: The Wind Beneath My Wings 185

Contents

On Birthings and Lessons and Holy Wisdom

One by one, day by day, the moments, the stories, the questions, the lessons appeared.

In the murky first light of dawn, when inky night is blotted at the edge with aubergine before it burns into tangerine, I'd tiptoe down the stairs of my old shingled house, not far from where Lake Michigan laps the shore. I'd click on the desk lamp in the room where I write—a room that once served as one-car garage, then maid's chamber, and now my book-lined typing hole—and I'd sit before the blank screen. By the time I cozied my bum against the hard plank of the chair, I'd surveyed the landscape of my yesterday and felt the zing of whatever moments had most captured my attention, my imagination, my heart. I knew which frame of the passing picture show begged to be plumbed. Nearly every day, there was some fragment of time— words shared, heart pummeled, triumph hard-won—that beckoned to be held up to the light. To be recorded. Questioned. Sifted through. Mined for any lasting lesson.

Sometimes I felt like a butterfly catcher—only my net was woven with words, and what I set out to capture, what I all but jammed in an old glass jelly jar for safekeeping, was as ephemeral as any swallowtail riding the southerlies: shimmering, brushing past my nose one instant; gone the next.

One by one, day by day, I was flailing at fleeting moments from the script of motherhood—nothing more complicated, nothing less complex than one heart hard up against another, one life literally in the hands of the other, a bond set from the start on a trajectory toward separation—in all its messy, primal, confounding, heartrending permutations. The one biological equation, genetic and soulful inheritance, from which there can be no escape. And therein lie its magnificence and its tug and its pull. And its possibility of infinite wisdom.

From the start, the moments that enveloped me most, the ones out of which the deepest inklings were born, were the moments that felt bigger, much bigger, than me. These were the moments that pulsed with questions that ultimately ask, how do we love? How, truly, do we love? How do we press against the bounds of what we thought our hearts could do and discover, blessedly, the capacity for more?

It was out of those moments and those few timeless questions—asked and examined from countless angles, across the arc of time—that I realized I'd stumbled onto a most essential curriculum.

To mother a child—by birth or by heart, by accident or happenstance or long-held dream—is to encounter love in ways never before beheld. In ways that stretch you, sometimes break you, build you up, and mightily and often demand the best that you can be. Lessons learned in motherhood's ineluctable front lines serve as a paradigm for loving far beyond our lifeblood. To learn to mother—to learn *from* mothering—is to learn to love in the ways of Jesus and Gandhi and Mother Teresa and Martin Luther King Jr. and even Louisa May Alcott's Marmee. It is to love as instructed in the Gospel, the Torah, the Qur'an, and every holy book ever inscribed: love as you would be loved.

I'd been a mother for more than a decade when I sat down to capture most of the moments gathered in these pages, ones that unfolded in my old house, in the hours I spent with or thinking about my two boys who happen to have been born eight years apart—a span dictated by years of heartbreak, by loss upon loss, years underpinned by long and bottomless stretches of doubt, and a fairly certain hunch that prayers and dreams "for just one more" might never come true. I'd been a journalist for a quarter century, and before that a pediatric nurse. A pediatric oncology nurse, to be precise. Which means I'd spent a good many years entwined with life and death. With paying attention. With asking and pondering sometimes impossible questions. And being left, too often, without the faintest answer.

It was in the alchemy of those hushed early-morning hours, before the staccato of the day quickened to *prestissimo*, when those three threads of me—mother, journalist, once and always a nurse—combined in ways I'd not anticipated: I was extracting moments of motherhood to ask the toughest questions, lay bare essential truths, and seize whatever shards of illumination I might have stumbled upon.

Always, my aim, my hope, my prayer, was to stitch tatters back into whole. To untangle. To mend what was broken, rubbed raw. Or to try, anyway.

Along the course of motherhood, I've studied hard the love lessons offered. In those first-light seminars of one, I attended the task with fingers to keyboard. I knew, because I'd practiced the craft in the pages of every day's news, that applying a journalist's steady eye, hard grasp, on the moment, the puzzle, the mystery, the conundrum at hand, it just might lead to epiphany.

I was intent on teaching myself how to love—unconditionally and without waver—in ways I'd longed to love and be loved.

Often, I wasn't too far into my maternal meanderings until I'd find myself tottering, breathless, lost—having arrived at some precipice, propelled by my own wobbly footed perambulations or my knack for getting snarled in cords of my own invention. So I did the one wise thing I know when nothing but abyss lay before me: I unreeled my prayer, set petitions to the wind, counting on those pleas to find the ears, the heart, the soul of Holy Tender God.

I prayed my way home, time after time.

And in the whisperings that stirred my soul and set me on my way, I did learn a thing or two. Learned what it means to love and love deeply. Learned how much it sometimes hurts. Learned just how brave I might be— if pushed, and if my kid's life (or heart or soul) depends on it.

Because I tend to live *ad maximum* as the ancient Romans would have put it, I've leeched every drop of heart and soul from my adventures in mothering. And my lifelong inclination for putting words to nearly everything that matters has left me with pages and pages of field notes from the trenches.

It was only in poring over those pages—a collection of life lessons that mostly span the decade that began when our older son, Will, was just thirteen, in his last year of grade school, and our younger one, Teddy, was five and new to kindergarten—that I figured out that what I'd culled was a real-time curriculum for loving.

Motherprayer

It's one that holds more questions, certainly, than answers. I think aloud. I pray. I fumble and stumble and sometimes skin my knees. I light candles and stir porridge on the stove. I lie awake night after night. And I leap from my bedsheets, determined to muscle on again.

I've wept. And laughed out loud. I've nearly crumbled under the weight of my worry. And through the grace of God, and saints and angels and a phalanx of wise and wonderful compatriots, I've tripped toward the light.

Maybe in thinking hard and deep and ponderously about the lessons that motherhood demands we struggle through, we might look down one day and see that our heart has grown deeper and wider and wiser than we ever imagined. Maybe we're one iota closer to the glorious magnificence we were meant to be.

Maybe we've learned from this one sacred heart—the heart of our child, from whom we can't, and won't, walk away—just how it might be to be fiercely and tenderly and infinitely loved, in that way that I believe we are loved by God almighty. And meant to love, most certainly.

Just maybe, in exploring motherhood, its interior and its borders, in illuminating the ledge where we let go and turn it over to the updraft I call prayer, maybe in imploring, begging, believing in the tender arms that will not let us—or our children—hurtle into the bottomless nothingness, we'll find God in depths and intimacies we've never known. Or imagined. God who loves us as a mother loves. God who hears the cries of our heart, from down the shadowed corridor, in deep of night. God who keeps the watch light burning, and will not abandon the vigil, not until we find our way through the darkness.

It's in knowing this God that we'll wrap ourselves more freely and more fervently in the shawl of prayer, motherprayer, those utterances that come from our most stripped-down essence. In knowing this God who is fluent in a mother's love, aren't we opening a channel that joins our heart to God's?

Motherhood, it seems, has caught me in its everlasting grip. No other instruction—sacred or otherwise—has so captivated, enchanted, or ignited me.

Nor so blessed me.

The Cradle That Is Prayer

Prayer, on my good days, is how I breathe. It's listening, as much as whispering. It takes the wobble out of my knees and puts the wallop into my heart's beat. It's woven into the hours, from cock's crow until the moment my eyelids finally flutter closed for the day. It unspools without measure or meter. It might be a geyser. Or merely a murmur.

The other morning, when I was deep in meditation, it came to me that prayer, at its holiest, is a cradle, woven from filaments of wonder and wisdom. Prayer, at its most powerful, perhaps, as transitive verb. Picture yourself swept into arms that hold you, that rock you, that lull you. Prayer, cradling.

Cradle, my dictionary tells me, is "to hold something gently and protectively." Etymologists, those learned folk who poke around in the vaults of centuries past for linguistic DNA, tell me the word has thirteenth-century Old English roots and trace its cognates to Old High German *kratto, krezzo,* "basket"; and German *Krätze,* "basket carried on the back."[1]

In the sixteenth century, the noun slipped into its form as a verb, and that's how I like it best. To be cradled. To cradle.

Isn't "to be cradled" to be rocked into sleepy-eyed quietude, to be harbored against harsh winds? Is that not a root of prayer?

And so I am—we are all—being cradled. Each and every day. Even—especially—the days when breathing comes shallow and rapid and hard, even the days when we're mostly holding our breath. We are cradled in great, tender arms that enwrap us. I particularly love the notion from the German *Krätze,* "basket carried on the back." Breathe that one in for a moment.

Might we be the basket carried on God's back? Might our cares, our worries, our rubbed-raw heartaches be hoisted onto shoulders far mightier than our own? "Basket carried on the back." Prayer, cradled.

Right in here—my life of late a blur of days whirling by so swiftly, too swiftly—I sometimes feel a wee bit light-headed, and my heart pounds so hard I worry, as I'm wont to do, that my not-so-ancient ticker just might give up the ghost. So, as if my life depended on it the other morning, I pulled myself out from under the sheets. And I tiptoed out to the holy cathedral just beyond the kitchen door, the one that vaults to the heavens, the one that on that morning was lit by a crescent of moon. Looked to me, more than anything, like one big eye winking at me. God's eye?

All around me, the dawn's soft, cool blanket fluttered, as if on a clothesline. The cardinals, cloaked in scarlet, were up and chirping away—it's fairly hard to beat a cardinal out of bed. The dew glistened. My toes took a bath when I tiptoed across the yard to fill the feeder with seed.

I stood there breathing. Feeling the arms wrap around me. Winking back at the moon. Then, I looked to my old shingled house, melted at the buttery light glowing from the kitchen. Sighed a deep sigh of thanks for the house that never fails to keep me safe.

I stood there for a short little bit, uncoiled my morning vespers, felt the soles of my feet sinking soft into the earth that holds us, always holds us. Then I puttered back toward the kitchen, where a lunch box awaited and, upstairs, a growing boy slept.

As I poured my first mug of coffee, I stopped to drink in a clutch of sunflowers that peeked from an old, chipped milk pitcher. I thought of the blessed, beautiful friend who had scooped up those wide-faced wonders from the farmers market. Then I climbed the stairs to wake the sleeping boy.

I pressed my cheek against his, longer than I usually do. I drank him in, my sweet sleeping child. And, as I'd been doing all morning, I leaned; this time, on him. I leaned on all of these wonders—winking moon, chattering bird, morning's dew pearled, old, blessed friend, and miracle child—and fortified myself for the hours to come.

I was cradled.

The cradle is there, always there. If we're willing to climb to the basket strapped to the back—the glorious, heavenly back—that carries us, even on days when we're dizzy.

Cradled is but one of prayer's verbs. Prayer plays out in a symphony of verbs. Many, many verbs. I've come to believe, over time and across the arc of keeping watch, in prayer of the transitive and intransitive ilk. Prayer in motion. Prayer put to muscle. Or imagination. Or heart. Prayer that deepens us, draws us to our core.

Never more so than motherprayer, a matrix of prayer in all its iterations that animates my every breath, most every rippled thought, and, more often than not, keeps me from plunging overboard.

My prayer today might cradle me. And it might come in the simple act of pressing cheek-to-cheek against my sleeping boy, a prayer of gratitude if ever there was. My prayer might come in counting stars, a prayer of wonder, always. For me, it's all a hodgepodge, no single stream of prayerfulness. No exacting measure. I simply know it's prayer when, as so often happens, I feel the mighty hand of God sprinkle goose bumps down my arms. When my leaden heart is lifted. When the door to the impossible is at long last unlocked, and hope comes rushing in.

The dilemma, though, is this: we live in a world where, too often, prayer—in any form—feels out of reach. Some of us don't have an inkling where or how to begin. The few lines we know, the ones we might have memorized a long, long time ago, fall flat. Miss the mark. And what about the hours when words won't come at all, when language escapes us? When we're enveloped by a hollow silence without end? It's suffocating emptiness, hopelessness defined.

Here, then, is a lifeline: we needn't find our way to the topography of prayer through words alone. In fact, sometimes, I think, we get tangled in the words, and the truest unfettered prayer is the prayer that catapults beyond scripted lines. How will I move into uncharted nooks and crannies of my soul if I merely grope along clinging hard and stubbornly to words?

What's most curious about this notion is that my whole life long—as far back as I can remember, to the days when I curled up on my braided bedroom rug with colored pencils and sheaves of schoolhouse paper and penned myself many-chaptered books, complete with line drawings, whole volumes secreted away in the shadows just beneath my old twin bed—my hungriest appetite has been for words. To this day, I toss back handfuls of words the way some might do with Milk Duds. I can suck on a single word the whole day long: *unspool, lollop, stippled, susurration,* pick one, any one;

each a concoction of syllables as delectable to me as a lemon sour might be to you.

I can't read a book without a pen, underlining, taking notes, scribbling every disinterred noun, every gut-punching verb into my all-purpose lexical repository, a stash known in the world of letters as "the commonplace book." It's a bulging-at-the-binding compendium of musings, scraps, and torn-out bits of wonder, wisdom, and plain old esoterica accumulated through a lifelong habit of hoarding. And it's ever-perched atop my old pine table, here where I do much of my typing. This compendium, you see, is something of a clearinghouse or storage bin, a catchall for ideas and persuasions. And this notion of stuffing wisps of knowledge into bound books is one with roots tracing to antiquity and coursing clear through the Renaissance, the American Revolution, and Y2K, to boot. Among the keepers of the commonplace book through time, you'd find Marcus Aurelius, Sir Walter Raleigh, Jonathan Swift, Thomas Jefferson, Henry David Thoreau, straight up to the newest millennium's Lemony Snicket. (One final digression: Seneca, the first-century Roman Stoic philosopher, likened the commonplace book to "a literary honeycomb," in which each cell—or line on the page—is swelled "with nectar sweet."[2] The nectar, of course, a flow in words, delicious words.)[3]

Words uncork welled-up parts of me, deep inside. Words put wings to my heart and soul, take me soaring. Words move me to tears. Words have been known to crumple me. I might spend the better part of an afternoon contemplating a single string of words, ones deliberately lobbed my way or merely snatched in passing. I daydream words. Pin them side-by-side, affix them as frilly French knots to plainspoken cross-stitched sentences, behold them for their singular capacity to take my breath away or merely tickle one of my fancies.

And yet, the undeniable truth, sad as it is, is that words—no matter how hard we try—can carry us only so far. And the destination I seek in prayer is one that lies far beyond the boundaries of language.

I've a hunch, a fairly certain one, that the native landscape of prayer—prayer at its deepest—is the one that sprawls on the far side of the chockablock of words. And once there, it's without boundary.

Prayer, if we pay attention, if we deepen, breaks out of linguistic binds. Takes flight. Bores deep. It's free-form verse. As near as our next breath. I've come to believe that prayer—the prayer I love best—is the practice of paying attention. And because I started paying close attention, I realized that for some of the holiest souls I know, prayer begins, prayer deepens, as they slip beneath the cloak of whatever is their prayerful verb of choice—baking bread, sowing seed and tilling farmer's field, daubing gold dust to oak plank in the icon writer's light-bathed studio, to begin to name the quotidian that transcends to mystical. It's the soulful discipline that opens the channel to the Holy, blocks out earthly distraction, sharpens, tightens focus, and culminates in meditative thrum, a *communion* with the Divine, one that honors the word's Latin roots, or as used by Augustine, in belief that the word was derived from *com-* ("with, together") + *unus* ("oneness, union"). Together, oneness.

I can't help thinking of Saint Francis of Assisi, who is famously said to have told his followers: Preach the Gospel at all times—if necessary, use words.[4]

Prayer might come in the act of tending a garden. Or keeping watch on the wilderness from high atop the forest ranger's lookout tower. Prayer, I've found, is what a farmer does when she genuflects amid the soybean rows and rattles away the hungry Japanese beetle. Prayer unfurls in soprano, offered up at the deathbed at the hour of someone's final breath. Prayer is what fills the heart as the midwife reaches for the newborn's crowning head and eases him into the holy light of delivery. Prayer, for me, is most often born of mothering.

It's what I breathed the night I climbed into the children's hospital ambulance and sped through miles and miles of city traffic to get my firstborn from a closer-to-home emergency room to the downtown pediatric ICU, in the long, dark hours after he broke his neck. It's what kept me, years later and more than once, on the telephone until the dawn came, when the one who placed the midnight call from college was the one who has long considered me his first and last line of defense. And it's just as certainly what percolates my joy when I slip a love note under a pillow or to the bottom of a lunch bag.

Mothering a child—the most sacred calling of my life—begs all I am and all I've got. And then some. Without the inside line to angels, saints, and Holy God, I'd not have made it, not even close, to labor and delivery. Nor a single day thereafter.

Motherprayer

Perhaps you already believe, as I do, that prayer is the hundred thousand little acts of kindness, of hope, of selflessness we stitch into the day. It's stirring porridge on a cold winter's morning for those we love, still nestled in beds. Delivering a piping-hot casserole, or a store-bought cake, to a lonely neighbor. Prayer is tucking a little one into bed. Talking over the long, hard day at the kitchen counter. Prayer is rolling up your sleeves and scrubbing a sick friend's bathroom floor. Prayer is at its glorious best when we soar beyond words. It's what we do and how we breathe.

Perhaps you've witnessed, as I have, how prayer seeps into our depths.

Sometimes, when I'm perched at the rocky edge, teetering toward the vast, inky pit that is despair at its darkest, or sadness or worry in gradations of gray, I lean into the one of which I'm sure: God. I take a lung-filling breath and rest against what I know to be tender and solid and always there—once I quiet the noise of my own making, that is. I begin, sometimes, with two simple words: "Take this." Or, maybe, "You there?" Then, as my breathing slows, I feel as if a hand is pressed against the small of my back, as if my shoulders are blanketed. I'm steadied. I'm filling—with hope and holy whisper. It's the whisper of God, gently tapping me upside the noggin and deep in the heart, reminding: *I'm here, right here. And I'm not leaving.*

Most of all, perhaps you, too, subscribe to the notion that prayer needs no words. That prayer sometimes is simply breathing. It is inhabiting the holy sphere where we know we're bathed in purest light. Where, as with a dear, dear soul mate, we can sit side-by-side, wrapped in silence. Rather than trying to wedge thoughts into syllables, we wordlessly drink in all that's around us. We marvel. We inhale. We listen. We imagine the sparks of the divine sinking deep down into the whole of us—lifting us up, keeping us afloat, leaning into the great, tender arms that are God's.

All of this is how and why we pray.

Prayer, a wise priest once told me, is practicing the presence of God.

Prayer, I'd add, is living, breathing motherlove.

And the prayer I pray most deeply, most often, is my unending loop of motherprayer.

Field Notes on Loving

On Field Notes

Field notes: *(n.)* When observing a culture, setting, or social situation, the term field notes refers to qualitative notes created by the researcher during or after observation of a specific phenomenon to remember and record the behaviors, activities, events, and other features of the setting being studied. They are to be read as evidence that gives meaning and aids in the understanding of the phenomenon.[1] As Harvard biologist Michael R. Canfield puts it: "Taking time to write out an idea or observation forces us to pause and consider."[2]

*I*n the realm of the naturalist, in the pages of those wisdom-filled illuminators who guide the bumblers among us into woodland and meadow and mountain and prairie, those who take us by the hand fording streams, pinpointing stars in the heavens, identifying species by song or feather or seed pod or number of stripes, the field note is at once necessary and generous. It is the account that details, elucidates what's before our eyes, and ears, and perhaps the whorl of our fingertips. Field notes capture the moment. Field notes are the scribblings we gather along the way. And, sometimes, someone else's field notes are the pages we riffle through when we come upon something we've not before encountered, the mysterious unknown. Field notes fill in the blanks. Field notes amplify the fine-grain, the barely noticed essential. Field notes erupt in "Aha!"

In the pages that follow, I've gathered my field notes. The notes I kept while keeping watch on the species I birthed. I compiled them—meditations on moments of motherhood, really—across time, an arc that begins with my first pregnancy and continues on to this day. I wrote them in real time—the eve of first grade, the first night my firstborn (with newly minted driver's license in his wallet) unlooped the car keys and loped into the dusky darkness, alone on the road in the old family wagon. I wrote of quotidian afternoons when the simple act of slicing a pear invited a moment of holy communion. And I wrote of the hollows in the weeks before and after we dropped our oldest at college—a thousand miles from home—when, for the life of me, I could not find my way in the uncharted landscape, the one that had stripped me of my place in his every day.

But rather than unspooling my field notes here in purely chronological order, I've done a bit of shuffling and gathering, gathering by theme as well as by years. To the front of the stack, I've pulled four meditations on the scant few bits that lie at the heart of mothering (for me, anyway): love like no other, courage beyond measure, unending prayer, and an all-embracing definition of mothering, the verb. One or two of those opening essays sweep across the whole of mothering and were written deeper and later into the journey, yet they belong at the fore, binding all that follows; sometimes, often, it takes time—and stumbling and skinning our knees and getting back up again—till we figure out what's most essential, maybe most obvious. From there, we turn back toward the beginning: we wend our way through some of the sorrows, the ones of infertility and miscarriage and loss that shatter our hearts. And we savor the joys, the tender soul awakening, the keen attention that so defines the art of mothering, the mother's apothecary of curative balms. Moving forward in time, we hold up to the light those moments when our children are inching toward the edge of the nest, taking flight—soaring, tumbling, soaring again. And, too soon, we're the ones with noses pressed to the windowpane, hearts swelled, longing. We're the ones poring over the frames of year upon year, asking how it all slipped by so swiftly, so before-we-were-ready. And that's when, perhaps, we look down and see that somehow along the way our heart has doubled or tripled—or more—in volume and depth and breadth and certainly in blessing. And the most emphatic prayer that spills from our lips is this: "Thank you. Dear Holy God, thank you and thank you and thank you."

Nest Building: The Scant Few Bits That Bind

Nest materials: Like a carton for store-bought eggs, nest materials help to cushion, insulate, and keep the clutch together.... Nest materials can be critical for some species, [adapting to bewildering diversity of supporting structures, and almost limitless in variety. Materials may include] stones and mud, animal and plant products, and human-made artifacts. [Adhesives—mud, saliva, caterpillar silk, certain plant fibers, even leaf mold—are essential for binding and architectural integrity in various nests.] These binding materials can be remarkably durable. For example, cellulose, the major constituent of plant fibers, is waterproof and, ounce for ounce, stronger than steel.[1]

Hormones and nest building: Passerines [birds that perch, comprising more than half of all bird species] may make more than one thousand trips to carry construction materials to their nests. Just what prompts such dedication has been the focus of numerous studies. Physiological ecologists have been piecing together how the complex practice of nest building is driven by hormones...and triggered by environmental factors... [starting with increased day length, the solar trigger].[2]

—*The Birder's Handbook: A Field Guide to the Natural History of North American Birds*

Nest weaving: Birds make good weavers because they use their beaks to push the thread through the fabric; they have well-coordinated head movements and good vision to follow the passage of the thread. The threads found in nature—grasses, plant fibers, and silk from spider webs and some caterpillar nests—are relatively short, only two or three times the length of the bird. So some birds make lots of knots to hold the fabric together. Sewing is used in nest building to attach pieces of material, such as two leaves.[3]

Nests: According to Aristotle, "Science is the union of knowledge and intuition and has for its subjects those things which are most precious in their nature." Nests are objects of art and also pure science, because each carries with it a complex and precious story of how and why.[4]

—*Architecture by Birds and Insects: A Natural Art*

Navigating the Landscape of the Heart

On Trial and Error and Love Like No Other

We come to this job, most of us, barely equipped.

Heck, I'd spent one fine summer down the lane, a summer girl of sorts, wrestling three lively kids into a daily schedule that, looking back, was a pure piece of cake. And I did have four brothers, one of whom was young enough that I might have been enlisted in occasional diaper duty. Maybe propped a bottle in his hungry mouth now and then.

And I did meander my way through nursing school. So that must have accounted for something. And I was the newsroom's default first-night babysitter, meaning that whenever the brand-new parents mustered the nerve to leave the newborn squaller for the very first time, I was the one employed to hold the fort. Keep monsters at bay. And, God willing, greet the nervous newbies at the door with babe in bundle, still breathing (and, there, I mean the baby—er, mostly).

Really, when I think about it, that's all I had on my résumé, in the little section labeled Work Experience, the part that should be scrutinized, amount to proof of passage, when you come panting to the double swinging doors marked Labor & Delivery. No Pretenders Welcome.

Once past that point, the only thing they make you do, really, is huff and puff, and finally someone yells it's time to push. So you push through the aptly named ring of fire, and then, like that, they hand you the little angel.

And that's often when it happens. You hear this head-jangling sound, I'd say it's a *schwoop*, like the sound of falling down a cave with the wind hurling against your eardrums. It's a moment, a deep-body whirl, that swallows you whole, and from there on in, you are in it forever and ever and ever. Amen.

It takes some bumbling in those early days, the ones when they set you loose from the hospital, the ones when you find yourself alone, in an empty kitchen, and there, in a bouncy baby recliner, one padded in many, many blankets, you have a screeching, squawking little bundle, one with scrumptious hands and thighs and feet, and fingers and toes you are tempted to nibble on.

You might consider, as I did in one rash, terrifying moment, returning said bundle to the store. Telling the nice shopkeeper that you really had no idea what you were in for and that you've decided this really isn't something you're cut out for. And besides, you need a potty break.

But then those mama hormones must kick in, the ones that indelibly etch that baby's wholeness into the whole of who we are. And from there on in, we're tethered—hook, line, and holy-ever-after sinker.

And somehow, from deep within, we begin the navigation of the voyage of our lifetimes. The one, for me at least, that makes all the rest fall by the wayside.

There has been, from the get-go, not another worry in my life that has mattered as deeply as the ones about my babies. I've lost countless hours of sleep—cradling them in the bathroom on frantic, fevered nights, tracing the source of lamplight that shone from the crack beneath a bedroom door at three or four or five in the morning, lying motionless under my sheets, frozen in my ruminations about what they have or haven't done.

But along the way, and time after time, I've felt the whoosh of heaven swirl around me, lift me up, and carry me for a ways.

When you commit to love in the way that a mama does—oh, she so deeply does—you come to taste a pure brew of oxygen that fills your lungs and puts flight to the flutter in your heart.

Say, when you're curled up on the couch with a pounding headache, trying to stay out of everyone's way, and suddenly, a sweet ten-year-old boy, one who's more inclined to dash up and down a soccer field, puts down his

TV clicker and comes to rub circles on your throbbing head. Then he goes to get a washcloth, something he's seen you do a million times. And he makes like he's the mama, taking care of you.

Or, when you are washed in worry about your college kid and whether he'll remember to turn in his final paper, and, out of the blue, as if he's tele-pathically picked up on your angst from all those hundreds of miles away, he calls you, from some river bank in the middle of who knows where, to let you know he's finally done it, turned in the darn paper. A mere three minutes before it was due, before he got docked a grade for dillydallying. And he calls just because he knows how hard you tried to keep a lid on it, and, at last, out of the mercy of his heart, he is loosening the noose that threatened to squeeze you bloodless.

Ah, yes, so go the lows and highs of this landscape we mothers learn to navigate by pure and repeated trial and error. Our pack list boils down to the merest few essentials: our full-to-the-brim heart, our ever-considering gray matter, every last muscle in our sometimes aching, exhausted bodies. And whatever else we need to employ to get the job done.

For the job, at its heart, is as fine as any life work could ever be: love as you would be loved. And love forever after.

"Always an Act of Courage"

On the Nonnegotiable Essential

*M*aybe it happens to you, too, sometimes. You are reading along, and words reach out like some sort of net strung between trees in a thick jungle. They entangle you, stop you in your tracks, don't release you for days and days.

So it was, as I was reading a news story about a cultural anthropologist who happened to be a single mother, when I stumbled onto seven words nestled inconspicuously into the rest of the sentences.

I read: "Motherhood is always an act of courage."

Just like that, it caught me.

As always, the best writing is stitched with wisdom. It catches you unawares. Elegant French knots of resonant truth threaded through the plain-sewn narrative.

One minute I was reading the life story of one brave single mother, the next I was entangled in a thought that would carry me for days.

"Motherhood is always an act of courage."

Indeed it is.

From the moment that seed of life burrows deep into the womb, makes its way to connect to the richness that is a mother's blood, lifeblood, that will feed, will sustain.

From conception on, there is no going back, if God is willing, if prayers are answered.

We move forth, one corpuscle tied to the next. We are in this, literally, together. Forever entwined. Though birth will begin the separation, there are ties deep inside that will never truly be cut, not with any knife.

From those blurry daydream days, before the labor comes, when in hazy, fuzzy terms you try as hard as you can to imagine this someone, to imagine how it will be.

It will be nothing like those dreams.

It will be nothing like anything you have ever known.

And the one sure thing, the only certainty, is you'd better tap deep into a tank of high-octane courage. No watered-down concoction can take you where you need to go. This trek has no road map and, too often, no shortcuts.

It's courage that will carry you around the tapered mountain passes, where the edge is steep, is precipitous. It's courage that will carry you through unrelenting passages, when you'd rather turn in swift retreat.

After all, they send you home with this squirming, hungry bundle—and no instructions attached. You shake as you sit in the backseat, the baby's father driving so cautiously you fear you might be rear-ended, the car behind you not understanding just how breath-catching a journey home this is, this long trip, the maiden voyage.

Then, the first morning you are left home alone with this babe, you break out in sweat. Or tears.

More often, both. The baby squawks, you try to figure out how in the world you will do this. How will you spoon the cereal into your own mouth, so you, in turn, can feed your screaming infant?

Courage? Oh, Mother Courage, you came to me, you filled me. Shaking, quaking deep inside. Uncertain, scared, somehow we carried on.

All along the way, it's darkness up ahead. We never know what might be around the bend. We simply keep putting one foot before the other.

How in the world can you take on the task of mothering if you are not filled up with courage? If you do not gulp it for breakfast, inhale it like undiluted oxygen?

I consider, in a slide show that makes me weep, the moments of courage of mothers I have known:

The mother, just this week, who watched her little girl's legs be strapped into braces—for a year.

The mother who kept vigil outside the operating room while oncologists poured hot chemo into her daughter's belly, a last-ditch hope to stop the entrenched cancer.

The mothers, so many mothers, who bravely step into the school conference room, where so many minds—and unknown faces—are gathered to map a plan to help the struggling child, the child for whom learning doesn't come in straight lines, or quickly. Or ever, it sometimes seems.

Or what of the mother who took the call from a stranger, who listened to the voice telling her that her bike-riding son had fallen, been found unconscious, limp and bloodied? That mother who drove, trembling, who carried her son to the emergency room, who listened as the doctor spoke words she'd never forget: vertebrae, high up in her firstborn's neck, were fractured, one for certain, another most likely. An airlift would be arranged.

And what about the less dramatic but no less daunting frame: the mother who drops off her child at the kindergarten door, who hears the cries from inside the room as she cowers in the hallway, barely breathing, wondering, how in the world will he make it—will she, the mother, make it—through the next endless hour?

I think of the mothers I admire most, the ones whose unbroken, unwobbling faith makes me stand straight, breathe deep, reach down and get a grip. I think of those mothers and realize every single one is a profile in pure courage.

You take on life itself when you bear a child, when you become a mother through birth or love or legal papers.

And when you cradle that child in your arms, rock him or her through the night, on the nights when fevers soar and cries grow shrill. And you are terrified, but you whisper to yourself, "This child needs me; stay strong. Don't waver."

I've been the mother who instructed my knees, "Don't buckle," when I thought they would, when I thought my firstborn's spinal cord was severed, when I overheard the tech (who'd just finished the three-hour MRI) whisper to a colleague, "It's really bad. I don't think the parents have been told." When I needed to wheel that cart-strapped kid down a long, lonely hallway, when I could not look into his eyes for fear of breaking down and falling into pieces. When I saw his life, and mine, pass before my eyes.

"…always an act of courage."

Is it not an act of courage, on any old school morning, when we wave our child down the sidewalk, watch him or her bravely board the school bus, when we know there are kids on that bus who taunt our child, who call him names, who make his school day an exercise in humiliation—and hell, besides?

And what of the times we pick up the phone, tell the principal in no uncertain terms that we will not let this go on?

When we walk up to the baseball coach, when we tell him that what just happened in the dugout was truly painful and that he had better make it right, for this is no way to model grace under pressure?

Even though, deep inside, we are shaking, quaking all the while. Not so practiced at this standing up and being counted. Except for when we look around, realize we're the one who's being depended on. We've become, after all, the grown-up. The one who will not let our children out in the rain, to fend endlessly for themselves, to march unshielded. We lift our voices, if need be. Make decisions. Stand taller than we've ever stood. Because it is our children for whom we are called to be more than we have ever been before.

I think back to my own mother of five who, at fifty, found herself a widow. Who huddled us by the door as we were about to step outside to the long, black car sent by the funeral home, who looked each of us in the eye and told us, "Make him proud," the father we would bury that morning.

It is courage—the hot wind of heaven that fuels our trembling wings.

It is courage—that makes us reach down deep and pull out muscle where we never knew we had it. It's where the backbone is. It's where, when we need to, we find the voice that speaks up, that won't relent, that settles only in solid resolution.

We are charged with much in this lifelong journey called mothering.

The one piece of armament sure to go the distance is the unfettered, unadorned, magnificent holy breath called Mother Courage.

And she comes to me through prayer, and prayer alone.

Motherprayer

On Sacred Mooring

*I*t is what we do on days like this.

We worry, yes. We scramble eggs. We pack lunches, thick with steak. We check on bedroom lights late into the night. Make sure they're off and tousled heads are sleeping. We drive. Deliver children to the schoolhouse door. And all day long, we keep an eye on clocks.

Short of picking up a pencil, slip-sliding into a school desk, and making like we're the ones who know the path to truth on the final exam, we really haven't many worldly options. Not in test-taking season. Nor any other season that makes the growing-up years a labyrinth that's laced with snap-traps and chutes and tippity ladders.

And so, we surrender.

We employ the mother tongue as ancient as any known. Since first birth (and I mean the dawn of time), I'd wager, there have been mothers who turn their words, their breath, their whispered vespers to the ineffable, the uncharted, the place where hope plays hide and seek.

We pray.

We fill in the blanks with supplications that wash out from deep inside us, and over us, and far into the beyond.

We pray for hours if we have to, keeping on with all the rest we do. Not letting on that there is prayer at work.

We drop to knees. We dab holy water, head and chest and shoulders, the sign of the cross. We lie down and stretch our arms as high as we can reach. We venerate. We call on God, and ones we love who are no longer but might well come to the holy blessed rescue.

Oh, yes.

I've seen heavy-hearted mothers, on their knees, crawl up great stone church steps and inch their way down a long, long aisle that ripped their flesh but not their spirit, dead-set they were on laying down their knotted, bundled prayers at the foot of a bare and marbled altar.

I've heard mothers ululate, sending untamed sounds to a place that understands, even if we've no idea just where that someplace is.

We pray, we mothers all, in many creeds and faiths and dialects, but always in one united tongue: we pray for our children.

We pray for what they need. We pray for what's beyond our reach, but so help us, we'll provide—if prayer can make it be.

There is an alchemy to prayer. A mysticism that cannot be explained. It is holy pleading raised to the nth power.

Motherprayer needn't be explained. We needn't pass a test. We can pray that children make it across the stage without tripping on their laces. And we can pray—just watch—that the blood test comes back clear.

This ordinary Thursday I was pulled, like lunar moth to lamplight, into the great stone church I always pass. Only, this morning, my footsteps fell into the dim-lit chamber, empty at that early hour. Only dawn's light poured through stained-glass windows, washed the floor in gem-dappled jigsaw puzzle. But that's not why I came.

I came, because deep inside my ever-Catholic heart I knew I could call out to my God and my prayers would be heard. I knew that each word I spoke would fall to God's feet, fall onto God's heart. And while I was at it, I put flame to wick, to one of the candles all squat in a row, a light that would burn through the day and the night.

It is motherprayer kindled. It is bathing, I am certain, the boy I love with all there is that I can't solely muster.

I scrambled eggs. I nestled steak inside the onion bun. I squeezed his hand. And kissed him on the head.

And then I watched him lope into the classroom, where three last exams stacked up like hurdles, the only thing between one long, hard year and summer.

Motherprayer

I knew, as I watched him go, that he wasn't all alone.

He is wrapped in motherprayer. And motherprayer is infinite and lasts forever.

Motherprayer picks up where earthly mother cannot reach.

Motherprayer is wholly holy. And holiness has ears, I've learned, for all that's spilled in never-ending prayer of mother.

Even if the Blessed One whispers not a sure reply, I always know the holy answers echo back to me and mine.

That's how it is with motherprayer. And that is why, on days like this, I pray with all my motherheart.

It's All About the -ing

On Mothering, a Verb Belonging to
All Who Practice a Particular Art of Loving

*M*aybe a proclamation would be the thing. Although that was done already. Maybe just some commonsense suasion could fix it.

It's about a little problem I have with that day carved out of the calendar, held up as Mother's Day. Far as I can tell, there's a missing syllable.

I would like to make the day not plain old Mother's Day, a noun. Which by my take is exclusive, too exclusive.

I would like to add an *-ing*. And make it Mothering Day, beckoning the verb. A day for all who mother.

Not just those who know what it is to have pushed the burning bulge as if your life depended on it. And not just those who've signed their name on someone's dotted line. Or stepped in without official papers.

All of that is fine. Amazingly, awesomely, only-MotherGod-could-have-invented-this, so very fine.

But there is more—there *are* so, so many more.

Yes, every last someone who has stroked a brow, wiped a tear, dabbed chocolate off a little cheek, fluffed a pillow, tucked in the covers, whispered bedtime prayers, set an extra place at the table, stretched a meat loaf, picked the peas out of the pasta salad, kissed a bloody knee, kept a retching tot from falling in the toilet bowl.

Yes, every pair of arms that's lifted a dead-weight child in the pool, played red rover until the cows came over, pushed a kid on training wheels around and around the block, turned the pages of *Goodnight Moon* so many times you find yourself chanting goodnight to the mittens when no one's in the room.

You get the point.

I have for years squirmed and wriggled when it comes to setting aside a certain Sunday, stockpiling loaves and loaves of toast that will be cut into triangles, smeared with jam and honey and cinnamon sugar, and delivered, teetering, on trays that stand a mighty chance of toppling off bedsheet-shrouded knees.

Not that I have anything against newspapers in bed or violets clutched in sweaty little fists.

It's just, gosh darn it, my world, for one, is highly populated with extraordinary motherers who have neither birthed, nor adopted, children of their own. And plenty who simply could not deliver, ever—they are men, for heaven's sake.

I am all for honoring the art of mothering. And I would make a motion to amend the noun and bow down before the brand-new ending.

The *-ing*, I argue, is where the emphasis should be. It's a verb—active, pulsing, life-propelling verb.

Long ago, when Julia Ward Howe composed her original Mother's Day proclamation it was all about women rising up and demanding an end to war.

That I could get in a froth about.

Especially the way she put it: "Our husbands shall not come to us, reeking with carnage, for caresses and applause. Our sons shall not be taken from us to unlearn all that we have been able to teach them of charity, mercy and patience. We, women of one country, will be too tender of those of another country, to allow our sons to be trained to injure theirs."[5]

So wrote Julia in 1870.

But, somewhere, the Hallmarks of the world got in the way. The second Sunday in May became less about the women of the world exerting their mother-ness on the global family, and more about fluffy slippers, hand-crayoned cards, and leaving whole chunks of the population to ache because, by accident of biology, they've not been able to get egg plus sperm to equal zygote, their unborn children never got to take a single breath, they've buried a child born from their own womb, laid a lifeless little body to rest—far, far too soon.

Aches, all, that never go away. All aches the second Sunday in May only serves to jab and pierce so stingingly I know women who barely make it through the day.

Or, perhaps, they're women who decided early on—or agonizingly— not to bring another soul into this blessed, broken world. Or men whose tender, caring touch goes uncelebrated, lost in all the hubbub of the third Sunday of June when to be a grill *meister* seems the height of all that matters.

They all mother, if not define themselves as mothers per se. If not their own children, then other people's children. Or the child who dwells in every single someone. Have you not been deeply mothered by a friend?

You needn't be with child, nor even be a woman, to mother, is my point.

I don't mean to be a grouch. And I hate to throw cold water on all the blessed moments the day will surely bring.

I just feel intent on proclaiming one not-so-little matter: may it be mothering, the art of tender caring, coaxing life, leaving mercy in your wake, the art that knows no gender bounds, no census-taker's definition, the art the world needs in mighty thronging masses, may it be mothering, and not just mothers, for which we stand and shout, "God bless you, each and every motherer."

From the Cookery Files...

When your morning prayer on a particular day—a day that demands much, too much, from its players—seems most aptly punctuated by the stirring of spoon through a muddle of oats. When the first thing you reach for, come dawn, is the grain that amounts to a mother's amulet. And as you stand there tossing in handfuls of shriveled-up gems—fruits the colors of amethyst, ruby, garnet, or onyx—you imagine yourself some sort of sorceress, arming your brood for the slaying of dragons to come.

Proper Porridge

I stand at the cookstove, stirring. And stirring. And stirring. Five minutes, maybe seven, bent in prayer. For that's what seems to happen every time I stand there, spoon in hand, circles upon circles lifeguarding the oats.

Oats + water + salt.

That's the equation. Quite simple. All the rest is alchemy, and stirring. Oats in the morning—oats done properly, I've found—unfold the day in slow time. Meditative time. If ever the cookstove becomes prayer altar it is at the dawn, when the house is only beginning its morning grunts and hisses and shivers and burps. When the kitchen is dark except for the flame of the burner and the single bulb that casts its faint beam on my pot.

I didn't used to stand at attention, not for so long a stir anyway. But then I went to Londontown, and one chilly morning I found a plump pot of porridge standing sentry on a shelf at a cozy corner cafe. I admit to being charmed by the name—*porridge* (poetic, with a hint of the ancient, the Celtic, perhaps; and as opposed to the more plebeian, American *oatmeal*)—as much as the contents lumped inside.

Then I dipped in my spoon. And what I tasted was pure soothe. If food has the capacity to sandpaper the rough spots of our soul—and I believe it most certainly does—then that first spoonful of proper British porridge declared itself "necessary balm." Balm begging to begin the day, every day. Or at least the ones when fortification is needed. When what lies ahead in the hours to come just might fell you, buckle your knees. And those of all the ones you love, the ones still dreamy in their beds.

While swirling the velvety porridge there in my mouth, I noticed the words on the cardboard tub in which the porridge was served. Again, a call to attention.

Here's what I read: "Well worth the wait: Porridge is a surprisingly tricky dish to perfect (it's taken us years to get ours right). Stirring is good. Boiling is bad. Slowly, slowly simmering is the key. You just can't rush a good porridge. So we don't."

It was cooking instruction as *koan*, as *kenshu* (Buddhist notions, both; the former a teaching, often a paradox or puzzle, prompting deeper enlightenment, the latter a way of seeing).

And it captured my attention, all right.

Worth-the-Wait Porridge

Provenance: Nigel Slater + Felicity Cloake + The Ballymaloe Cookbook

Yield: 2 bowls, or I if you find yourself famished after a long night's nap

I cup rolled or steel-cut oats*
3 cups water**
¼ teaspoon salt
Assorted accoutrements: dried cranberries, apricots, raisins; sliced banana, chunks of apple; handfuls of almonds or walnuts; a spoon of peanut or almond butter; a sprinkling of wheat germ; a drizzle of honey or molasses; a spoonful of brown sugar. (Any of these would likely

leave a porridge purist aghast, but some mornings a bit of rabble-rousing *is* the order of the day.)

* Porridge *cognoscenti* all prescribe Flahavan's Irish Porridge Oats, if you're aiming for indescribable deliciousness.
** While water is traditional—in fact, *The Scots Kitchen*, F. Marian McNeill's recently republished 1929 classic, recommends spring water—porridge is sometimes made with hot milk, although that might mark you as a sybarite.[6]

After culling dozens of porridge recipes, I've determined that all the enlightened porridgers subscribe to a quick toasting of the oats, a mere minute or two in a dry porridge pot over medium heat, until faintly golden. (If you choose steel-cut oats, or a mix of rolled and steel-cut, you'll want to soak the steel-cut bits overnight, after pouring boiling water, in three-to-one ratio, water to oats, atop the oats, and parking them off in the corner. Put the lid on the pot, and bid them goodnight.)

Next morning, or when your belly's growling for that proper porridge, add water to oats in the pot (unless you've gone for the overnight soak), or if you prefer your oats creamier, make it milk or even cream. Whichever your pleasure, keep to that three-to-one fluid-to-oats ratio, your golden ratio here. (If you've opted for the all-night immersion, you might need to add just a glug of water or milk in the morning so your oatsy bits are sufficiently aswim. But after a long night's idle, your steel-cut bits likely will need little but heat at this point. And fret not: oats might be the original forgiving grain.)

Stir, on low heat. A good five to ten minutes, please. Yes, stirring without pause—long, slow, meditative circles with your wooden spoon, or spurtle, a flat wooden stirring utensil designed by the Scots in the fifteenth century to keep oats from going lumpy, but of course. (Opines Mr. Slater: "Stirring is essential if the porridge is to be truly creamy."[7])

Add salt after porridge has been cooking for a good five to ten minutes. (Again, notes Nigel: "If the salt is introduced too early, it can harden the oats. Porridge needs cooking for longer than you think if the starch is to be fully cooked.")

Put the lid on your porridge pot and remove from the heat. Allow the velvety mound to breathe deeply and surrender to its steamy confines. A five-minute rest at a minimum. There is simply no hurrying a porridge of proper production.

Ladle into your favorite bowl, douse with a splash of fresh, cold milk, and adorn with handfuls of whatever accoutrements brighten your morning. Or to put it as the British food scribe Felicity Cloake so poetically puts it in *The Guardian* of London (and why wouldn't you want to put it thusly?): "A girdle of very cold milk, or single cream on special occasions, is essential...but a knob of butter, while melting attractively into the oats, proves too greasy for my taste."[8]

Mourning: When the Nest Is Barren

Birds and mourning: "A paper in the journal *Animal Behavior* presented a study about Western Scrub-Jays [and their so-called] funerals....Researchers placed several objects, including pieces of wood, stuffed scrub jays, stuffed Great Horned Owls, and dead scrub jay carcasses, into people's backyards to observe how the neighborhood scrub jays responded. [The jays ignored the wood and menaced the imposters.] Intriguingly, a prostrate dead jay [elicited a] high number of calls [that drew] in other scrub jays from afar. [While the jays noisily clustered around the dead bird, they decreased] their foraging for food in the area for over 24 hours....It is completely unscientific to draw a conclusion that animals grieve in the same way we humans do, but it's equally unscientific to state that they don't." So wrote Laura Erickson, former science editor at the Cornell Lab of Ornithology. When asked about birds' response when a nest is attacked or shaken from a limb, and eggs or young are lost, she replied: "Birds don't have the luxury of a protracted grieving period during the nesting season. Every day they put off re-nesting gives the next brood a poorer chance. It's a tough world."[1]

Tea for Two,
a Dream in Shards

On Finding Our Way Through Grief

I would have wanted her to have one.

We would have poured each other violet-colored waters and nibbled on chrysanthemum-petal canapés. We would, perhaps, have slipped on alabaster gloves, mine sizes larger than hers. And, giggling, I would have taught her to lift and curl her pinkie, just so, just as my mother had once instructed me.

That is what mothers and daughters indulge in, afternoons of make-believe teas and the whisperings that go with them. That is where secrets are shared and the beginnings of dreams are spun, all purled by the tinkling of little teacups against little tea saucers, and the lifting of the teapot's lid, and, of course, the spooning of sugar lumps from the bowl that is their own.

And so it was, that dream that shattered into so many pieces, that held the crux of my sorrows.

My little girl didn't get to sip her first make-believe tea. My little girl didn't get to be born. She died after only three and a half months in my womb, and when she was gone from my everyday I wanted achingly one thing: to make something that would forever be hers and mine alone, to make it with my hands and of the earth, and to make it something that could be steeped, like a good Earl Gray, in the rich vapors of imagination.

Motherprayer

I wanted to make her a tea set, a tea set in miniature, fitting for so tiny a baby as was my little girl.

Yes, I was pulled to the pottery table by my heart and the ache in my palms that could never again hold her close.

And there, in a clay-spattered studio housed in what was once a livery stable, I perched my heavy heart on a potter's stool.

I'd signed up for a Sunday afternoon's class—thank you, Lord, for such serendipity as an ad that captured my heart's desire, a class that promised I could make in one sitting a miniature set for tea.

And so, the crude lump of gray clay laid before me, I started kneading through the strata of sorrow with my thumbs and my palms. Every once in a while even that pinkie made itself useful, holding firm the base of a thimble-sized cup. As formlessness gave way to a spout and a handle, and a lid that actually fit on its perch, I felt some sort of giving-way of grief.

There was even whimsy as I furled snakes of clay into handles and tops for my cups, my cookie platter and, my *pièce de résistance*, the pot. My heart bobbled more when I surveyed the tubs of available paint and picked for my little girl's tea set a brilliant cobalt blue and yellow the color of lemons. I'd wanted sunshine, but lemon had to do—you get what you get when yours is the last class of the weekend.

And then it was finished, not perfect, not without dribbles of paint and wobbly handles, a fitting end to my labor, so like life itself, so especially now. Tears washed finally over my tea set; they wouldn't stop and I couldn't bring myself to try. I was letting go of something so much bigger than my pot, my platter, my cups, and my bowl.

I had to leave it all there to be fired, I found out, and the pang of not wanting to leave yet another something behind was not a little thing. It should be ready any day now, my cobalt blue set with the lemon sunshine beaming from its platter.

Maybe, just maybe, there will come an afternoon when I pluck chrysanthemum petals from the garden and sprinkle violet drops into a teapot of water. And I will raise a cup to the heavens and, just for the love of it, curl my pinkie just so.

Growing a Heart: Follow the Numbers

On Tracing a Timeline of Hope

*E*very time I dig through my wallet, there it is, the little stack of Post-its, paper-clipped and worn, right between the Kinko's copy card and the quote from a great man that I once scribbled on the back of a receipt.

It has been there nearly six years, the paper-clipped wad. It'll be there forever, I think. It's one stack of papers I cannot, will not, throw out.

In the tiniest penmanship I could possibly have penned, I once made a chart I checked, oh, twenty times a day, nearly every day, for nine months. I was pregnant then, with the unknown person who became my little boy, and so enthralled was I with this majestic creation that I had to make myself a way of marking off the unseen unfolding inside me.

It begins: "14 days—heart beats; 26—arm buds; 28—leg buds; 30—¼-½" long, beginn. umb. cord."

It was my way of tracing, in numbers and dashes and my own abbreviations, the course of the life forming inside me. It was my way of picturing every blessed step, culled and copied from a physiology book too fat to lug around, left over from my days as a nurse. I wanted to watch, if only in my mind, this unbelievable spectacle of life.

Maybe, too, it was because I knew what it was to not even get to follow the numbers. I'd had the joy once before of watching the plus sign turn pink, only to then wait and bleed and cramp, and get rushed to surgery, and wake up with a triangle of scars, no baby, and a missing fallopian tube. This time, maybe, somehow, if I could guide my finger down the days, I could keep it from falling off the track.

So I made myself this little graph to follow along, barely able to wait till I got to the next line of scribble, the next great stride in the making of my baby.

I would pull it from my wallet on the train. Peek at it during my work-day. Stare at it at night, marveling, rubbing my belly, while my little paper put me in touch with the greatest miracle I had ever known.

I followed it right through to the last line on the two-by-two-inch square, the one that read, "8-9 mos—gains 4, stores protein."

Not long after that, eight pounds nine ounces of protein and muscle and bright blue eyes landed in my arms, my pieces of paper come to glorious life.

Still I kept my paper-clipped timeline right where it had always been, in the dark of my wallet, where I could still peek and remember the waiting, the breathless expectation.

It became my talisman; if it stayed there, where it now belonged, maybe it would carry me through another miracle, allowing me to finger it and to hope.

Two more times I would get a chance to begin again at the beginning, to read, "14 days—heart beats," but the first of those times I never peeked again after "3 mos—moves body parts, swallows, practice inhale and exhale."

That was my little girl. I held her for a moment before she slipped out of my hand, the size of a string bean but perfectly, gorgeously human, those arm buds and leg buds and a face I'll never forget.

The time after that I didn't even get that far, and I never got anywhere again, no matter how hard the doctors tried, no matter how much I prayed nor what I promised God.

My one little miracle is almost five now, and throughout my life I find scattered scraps of hope I was unwilling to give up. There are baby seats I swore I'd get one more chance to use, now stuffed under the stairs. There are cardboard books I thought might submit to another round of teething, and even dusty old parts of a breast pump I thought I'd once again get to loathe.

I can't even bear to look in the boxes of baby clothes whose every stain and worn seam I know by heart.

You see, I always thought I'd have a gaggle. I never would have guessed I'd only once see my belly swelled and beautiful with life.

So I held on tight, so tight, to every little thing that goes along with having a baby, carrying a baby, feeding a baby, teaching a baby, loving a baby with your whole heart.

It was as though, if I kept the things around me, the chance of having that baby somehow wouldn't slip away once again through my trembling fingers.

But time teaches lessons, even lessons we don't want to learn.

I am starting to think that maybe, just maybe, I should pack up the essentials of babyhood and pass them along, as I did my last prenatal vitamin, to someone blessed to be with child.

I, too, am blessed. If the chart I scribbled long ago had continued to today, it would read: "5 yrs—fills yr heart by the hour, takes yr breath away."

Postscript: In the winter of my 44th year, eight years after my firstborn, I had a dream that woke me from my slumber. I distinctly recall every detail, even now: a woman in a navy cable-knit sweater looked me in the eye, in the thick of a noisy crowd, and, stirringly, insistently, declared, "You are pregnant."

Her words, an annunciation really, shook me from sleep and prompted me to elbow awake my husband in the middle of that night, though by daybreak he wouldn't remember a word of it. Nor did I mention it again, except hours later when I finally whispered the whole of it to my best friend who happened to be spending the weekend, in town from New York.

I insisted to my friend that it was impossible, a cruel taunt at best, that all my doctors had told me four years earlier to give up hope. By then I'd had an ectopic pregnancy, three miscarriages—including a baby girl with trisomy 13, a chromosomal anomaly that stopped her heart after three and a half months in the womb—and a few complicated rounds of fertility boosters. After all that heartache and hoping, I'd finally made peace with being the mother of our one and only.

Yet later that very afternoon, at my friend's unrelenting urging, I halfheartedly trudged to the drugstore to buy one of those fancy little home pregnancy tests, the sort that flashes a pink plus sign if the answer is yes. It flashed pink, all right.

I let out such a shriek as I yodeled my husband up to the bathroom, where I stood quaking, that he'd later tell me he swore he must have left a really big blob of toothpaste in the sink.

As is our classic Catholic-Jewish response, I dropped to my knees in an emphatic sign of the cross, and his first words were, "I think we should go to the synagogue."

And, against all odds, on the hottest August night of the summer of 2001, as I barreled toward 45, I birthed eight pure pounds of Dream Come True, Prayer Answered. He is to this day the one I think of as "The Egg That Wouldn't Take No for an Answer." I refer to him often in these writings as my "little one."

Mama Altar

On Holding Up Our Sisterhood of Sorrows

*I*t started as I drove home from the grocery, my eyes stinging with tears. I'd gone in to grab some orange juice, a perennial thirst in this house. Ran into Addie, my friend who runs the front end, who over the years, as she's rung up my eggs, shoved my gallons of milk down the beltway, has filled me in on her longing, her longing to please grow a baby. All around her it seems, everyone else is getting good news, getting pregnant. Not Addie. She, nearly 40, has had month after month of the no news that is very sad news in the baby department. As we talked, I wiped a tear from right by her eye, her beautiful, beautiful eye.

Then I drove home, crying too.

I know what it is to bang on the locked gates of heaven and feel like nobody's home, nobody's listening. I know what it is to want, more than anything, the round lump of baby in your so-aching arms.

Just a few days before the grocery, I'd walked into a quite crowded room but could not miss the light beams shining from a friend. A friend who this time, for the first time, wore a billowy top that shouted, without hesitation, "I'm pregnant. I'm waiting."

The beam on her face reminded me of ones I'd once worn. I couldn't help—again—my own tear or two, moved by the joy of remembering. But as we talked I found out she, too, knew what it was to hold her deep breath. She'd lost one little girl, and she was scared, scared to trembling, that she could lose this one too. Not that there was any reason she would. Just because she's a mama who's been there. And once you're there, it's terribly hard to not think you'll land there again.

I've been in that place myself. Know what it is to behold a miracle round your middle. Know what it is to hold your breath for nine very long months, so afraid that the miracle could slip away. I, too, had lost a little girl. Once stared at the fuzzy gray lines of a baby stone-still in my womb. Looked into her face as she slipped through my fingers. Left her behind in a little wood box, dug into the earth on my papa's own grave, in the drizzly cold of a cemetery, years and years ago now.

I know the dark and the light of fertility. I know its abyss and its mountaintop. I know the breathlessness of the ascent and the gasping for air when you're pushed off the trail.

I am forever a woman whose heart was seared by the loss and the triumph of childbirth.

I am, I'm afraid, a card-carrying member of the sisterhood for life.

And you do not abandon your sisters.

You build them an altar. You say a prayer, yes. But, even more, you build a prayer tableau and you take it to the next power.

You gather the makings of your prayerful intentions, the physical manifestation of what you are asking. It's something that women, indigenous wise women, have been doing for ages. I have such a friend, one who makes house calls with bundles of sage and feathers and nests, and she's taught me. My mother, who builds May altars, has too.

The altar is there when you're not. It's there when you wander past, reminding. Nudging: *Whisper a prayer. Don't forget. Don't leave those women alone. Hold them close in your prayer.*

And so, spurred by those faces, one in deep longing, the other in deep hope, I came home and started to gather.

I gathered talismans of hope and believing. Of my own dreams that had finally come true. I pulled from my top drawer the little pregnancy test, the one that I've kept since the cold afternoon when the plus sign turned pink and my dream that would never come true, started to come. I reached in the drawer by my bed, lifted the name bands of delivery, one for mama, one for baby. I plucked the most Blessed Mother of all. And a gold-winged angel, to boot. I snatched a few tulips from the kitchen, decided blood red was a color quite apt. I even remembered the tiniest prayer book, one that once was my mother's. And then I laid them all on a rectangle of lace made by the grandma I never knew, the one who, at forty, gave birth to the man I called Papa.

I made an altar for the would-be mamas. The two I know and the hundreds and thousands I don't.

We are a sorority who share a particular pain, often unspoken. Sometimes you haven't a clue who your sisters are.

But once you've been where they are, you can never again look into the eyes of a woman afraid, a woman desperately longing for life, and not join her brigade.

You pray, and you pray mightily. You get down on your knees. You beg at the locked gate of heaven. You make deals, if you have to. And you pray to God that you do not hear only the echo of your deep incantation lost in the canyon of No.

You know what it is to hear the sound of your heart cracking. You do not leave a mama abandoned. You do not leave her to tremble, to quiver alone.

You muster the force deep inside you. You envision a babe, safe and asleep, in her arms. And you pray to God that someone is listening, someone comes through for those mamas.

If there is a sorority of promise, you are signed on. Forever, for life. And so I bow down at the altar.

From the Cookery Files...

When the civilized art of taking tea entreats, and the cookie platter begs to be heaped with concentric circles of sweets. When not any lump of plebian dough will do, because the occasion is intended to lift a leaden heart, to stitch together the brokenness that life too often brings, or simply to infuse a jolt of unsuspected joy into an otherwise humdrum day.

Teatime Tuffets

In my storybook imagination, I sit down to afternoon tea with steamy pots of chamomile and platters of delicate cutout Linzer heart tarts, those peekaboo windows of almond-rich cookie, the tops and bottoms cushioned with jam and dusted with confectioner's powdery drifts. But the truth is, I'm not such a precisionist, not in the kitchen anyway; I'm more of a slap-dasher. I live to improvise. A splash of this. A *soupçon* of that. Which isn't what's called for in the baking department. There, where we roll out the well-chilled dough and employ the menagerie of tinware cutters, we need patience. And fine motor skills that escape me.

Which brings me to my tea nibble of choice: the raspberry thumbprint nest. A plump tuffet of buttery dough, rolled in a collar of smashed bits of pecan, impressed with a thump of my thumb, dolloped there in the thumbwell with a spoonful of raspberry delectability. Looks to me like a robin's nest in the springtime, a likeness that puts flight to my heart. And all that rolling and pressing, it's an excuse to play with your food, disguised as pastry making.

And so, in the teatimes I wish I'd had with my little girl, and in the countless ones that animated my long-ago days with both of my boys, when a company of stuffed bears plopped down to join us, I opted more often than not for the roll-'em-and-press-'em delight, the raspberry thumbprint. In a pinch, when teatime was beckoned with little notice, I reached in the pantry (always stocked) for that tried-and-true emergency backup, Pepperidge Farm's Gingerman cookies, adorable crisps that quite nimbly prance across the tea tray. Or nearly as grand as a thumbprint, Walkers Pure Butter Shortbreads, easily dunked in a vat of raspberry jam or preserves (a store-bought move that approximates the thumbprint in taste if not adorableness, and thus has rescued many a tea from the brink of sweets deprivation).

Raspberry
Thumbprint
Nests

Provenance: Jean Paré's Company's Coming: Cookies +
Land O'Lakes Butter back-of-the-box recipe

Yield: 40 cookies

I cup butter, softened
½ cup brown sugar, firmly packed
½ teaspoon almond extract
2 eggs, separated
2 cups whole wheat flour
I teaspoon baking powder
¼ teaspoon salt
I cup chopped pecans
½ cup raspberry jam

Preheat oven to 325 degrees Fahrenheit.

Cream butter and brown sugar; add almond extract; beat in egg yolks.

In separate bowl, combine flour, baking powder, and salt; add to butter mixture and mix well.

Form dough into 1-inch balls; dip in egg whites to coat; roll in chopped pecans; place on ungreased baking sheet 2 inches apart.

Here comes the fun part: press your thumb into the middle of each ball of dough, making an indent and creating your own little nest shape.

Bake for 5 minutes.

Remove from oven and quickly press the indents again with your thumb; return to oven and continue baking for 10-15 minutes. (Keep close watch; once the edges begin to golden, you'll want to grab your oven mitts and rescue the nests.)

Remove from the oven and fill indents with jam while cookies are still warm.

Cool completely. Tuck in cookie tin (with lid) lined with wax paper for safekeeping, up to three days. Or perch atop your favorite cake pedestal and ferry to the tea table. It won't be long until there's nothing but crumbs and the vivid memory of tea for two (or more) hearts.

Hatchling: Tender Soul Awakening

hatchling: (*n.*) a very young bird that has recently hatched from its egg, and not old enough to take care of itself.[1]

Hatching: The developing embryo is protected by the egg's hard chalky shell, composed almost entirely of calcium carbonate crystals stabilized in a protein matrix, which provides strength and makes the shell less brittle. It's porous, meaning air and moisture can pass through, with as many as 30,000 tiny pores on an emu egg, but a mere 300 on a wren's egg.[2] The shell is ingeniously adapted to bear the weight of an incubating parent, conserve moisture, and shield from predators. Yet, it presents a predicament: how to get out? First, the chick develops an "egg tooth," a soon-lost calcified nub that pecks away at the inside of the shell, and "pipping muscles" at the back of the neck, adding oomph to the pecking, or pipping. Birds begin chirping before they break through the shell, a miraculous thing to behold, the soft sound of peeping from inside an unhatched egg.

In most species hatching tends to occur in the morning, possibly because it allows time for a feeding before nightfall. It appears that the alternation of day and night is perceived within the egg, thus permitting the chick to hatch at the best possible time.[3]

—*The Birder's Handbook: A Field Guide to the Natural History of North American Birds*

Teaching My Firstborn to Pray

On Sacred Whisper at the Heart of Childhood

I got on my knees the night of the day I saw the little white spot on the ultrasound.

The spot was blinking. It was my baby, my first.

And I knew there was only one conversation that was going to get me through to the end. The one I'd already begun with the maker of that baby. I mean God, of course.

Besides the umpteen times I checked in all during the day, begging for this, promising that, there was only one way I ended my day, no matter how rag-doll limp I felt by the time my pillow was an arm's reach away. I got on my knees. I whispered my heart's every fear, praise, and promise. And every night I ended with my grand-slam petition, the one I thought covered it all, got to the heart of the matter. "And, dear God, please make this blessed angel the light of your love in this world."

I wanted my baby to all but glow, to be the candle this dark world some days so needed. I wanted health, yes, four limbs, you bet, but I'd take whatever I got, just so long as my little baby was a spark of the divine in our midst.

That prayer, the last anointing of my unborn baby's every day, was—for years and years, until he was old enough to wriggle out of his bedtime's ministrations—among the last utterances that fell upon his ears as he settled into sleep.

The night of the day he was born, buzzed on the high of my life, I nestled him next to me, stared into his dark blue eyes, ran my fingers over every bare inch of his skin, laid my hand on his so-perfect head, and whispered as tears coursed my cheeks, "Dear God, please make him the light of your love in this world."

And so it went, night after night, lying there, nursing him, talking him to sleep, I began the prayer that was a litany of thanks in three parts: for every little body part, for everyone who loved him, and for every little thing that had happened to him that whole long day. He never went to sleep without hearing those words, always ending with the bit about the light of God's love in this world.

I was teaching my little boy to pray. Teaching him that every little breath was a gift. Teaching him, night after night, as I touched his fingers, his toes, his hands, and his arms—naming the names as I passed over each part, head to limbs to trunk—that this was who he was, and none of it was to be taken for granted. He drifted to sleep with a mama whispering a mantra, rhythmically touching and naming all of who he was.

Every night he was lulled by the incantation, until one night he began, in his little baby voice, to repeat after me. He was learning to talk; he was learning to pray. Ticking through the list of thanks for the day—for the little moments, the heartaches, the joys—we sprinkled holiness on all that had unfolded from daybreak till dusk. Thank you for leaves that crunch, for mashed potatoes made by Grammy, for just-born stars twinkling in the sky.

He learned that all things matter. He learned, I hope, that words matter, too, and saying thank you is not to be pushed aside. Most of all he learned that God is the unseen, but very much present, Someone to Lean On in our house.

That's what I always wanted—for him to know with his every breath that there was a God to whom he could always turn, with whom he could share every twitch and twang of his heart.

My sweet boy is growing up in a house where God comes in two religions, Catholic and Jewish. And while the traversing of that landscape is uncharted, and sometimes steeper than suspected, I've always rested easy in the knowledge that one path for my child would be clear as could be. He could talk to God, my sweet child could. I could carve for him the course straight to God. I could try, anyway.

In time, he took over the bedtime riffs on his own. He spelled out all that there was to be thankful for, the wrap-up of his kindergarten day, then first and second grade and beyond. Mostly, he preferred to be my echo, letting me tick through the day's thanks, winding it up with both of us, and sometimes his papa too, blowing kisses to God—out the window or flung toward the ceiling—along with a promise (or is it a plea?)—"Good night, God, see you in the morning."

One evening, after the little fellow (a kindergartner at the time) wrapped up his pre-dinner spiel, "Thank you, God, for this food and for everyone and everything in this world," we somehow stayed on the subject of prayers. Stuffing a baby lettuce leaf in my mouth, I asked, "Do you ever talk to God during the day?"

"Oh, yes," he said, as matter-of-factly as if I'd asked if he ever needed his shoes tied. "When I'm on the playground and I'm about to put my legs through the rungs, I say, 'OK, God, give me courage.' And then I jump."

Oh, yes. My little boy had learned how to pray. He was off on his own, my heart told me. It's taken, I thought, the seed I planted so long ago, it's sprouted. And never could I have imagined how glorious it would feel to let go, to stand back and watch him soar.

My prayer, it was answered.

Indeed.

Monster Fighter

On Chasing Away What Makes Us Tremble

*M*y little one plays a never-ending game of dot-to-dot all day long. He changes socks, he drops them. He yanks off his shorts, he leaves them puddled on the rug. You could trace his every move, his every change of clothes and plaything, walking room to room, plucking from the floor, where he has deposited all the evidence.

We are trying to change that. We are in week 3 of pick-up therapy.

Thus, when I wandered in his room the other night, en route to his least desired destination—bed—I was (a) not so surprised to see the detritus of a busy day strewn around the rug and (b) insistent that it return from whence it came: the basement.

He truly is a good little boy, but this night my pointing down the stairs was met with unblinking resistance.

"It's for fighting monsters," he informed me. "I'm wearing it to bed."

It seems that while I was wiping out the sink one last time for the evening, tucking ice cream spoons away, he was carefully, premeditatedly, scouring the basement for the very tools I had thought were mere droppings from the day.

He had climbed up stairs with hockey stick and batting helmet, swimming goggles, and, of course, his trusty saber. The one that glows and makes a throaty roar. More like a gargle, really, but don't tell that to a five-year-old monster warrior.

And so, after brushing all those teeny-tiny baby teeth, not a one of which is even wiggly, he pulled off the ordinary clothes of ordinary mortal, and, like Superman inside the phone booth, became the Monster Fighter boy.

The goggles went on first. "Monsters poke your eyes out," he once again informed me, matter-of-factly, as if he'd been reading monster manuals and I had not.

Step 2, according to those manuals, I suppose: the batting helmet. Backward, apparently. Giving the monster warrior a Darth Vader sort of style. Perhaps he'd been preening before the mirror, trying it front and back. Or perhaps these things just happen. Perhaps little boys just know what it takes to trounce a scary thing in bed.

The light saber, curiously, wisely, was clipped onto the elastic waist of the undies. This, he'd decided, gave him maximum monster-battling maneuverability.

Then, the hockey stick. This, oddly (as if all the rest weren't odd enough), he threaded through the undies, on a fierce diagonal, wholly crossing his little body. He slid one end, the end that doesn't slap the puck, down behind the waistband on the left, poked it out the leg hole on his right. Hmm.

Somehow, carefully, I assure you—boys, again, know instinctively to be careful in these particular ways—he climbed abed.

And there he lay, armed and very ready for whatever purple, hairy, green-fanged thing dared to cross his threshold.

So fierce he was, lying there, eyes like frog, head in turtle shell, sticks at the crisscrossed ready, any monster who came his way would simply have to be a fool.

This monster gear has been a part of bedtime for the whole last week. Every night there is the slightest tweak in the armament. The helmet and the sticks, though: indispensable.

It didn't take me long to connect the dots, to draw the line, between monster-fighting nights and end-of-kindergarten days.

Aha, I said, as I played assistant to the ever-delicate ascent to bed, a climb that could, with just a single sorry twist, impair his future. If you catch my drift.

Of course I said in the most nonchalant way what I always say of monsters: They aren't real, sweetheart. They are pretend. Monsters live in books and on the TV screen.

Motherprayer

I did not press the point because surely there is something he thinks he needs to fight. And I'll always honor that. Honor the existence of whatever unnamed hairy monster lurks inside his head.

If only you and I could so simply fight our demons. If only sliding on a hard-shelled helmet, squeezing on the safety goggles could shield us from our fears. Instead, we pray—pray heartily.

I am thinking that the end of school is feeling a bit like walking off a cliff or into a big, dark cave. It is a darkness, an unknown, that we step into every day. But we aren't five. So we hide our safety goggles. Keep the helmet under our hat. Don't let on how mightily we quake.

When you're five, though, you hide little. You strut your safety gear. It's just the monster outlines that remain a little fuzzy.

In fact, my monster fighter is not saying much about these monsters. He is keeping the enemy rather under wraps, close to the vest. A good monster warrior is like that. He can't disclose too much about the enemy.

All we know is that the enemy is there. And the monster warrior is armed and ready. And being very brave. He'll not slip blindly into the night. He is safe, I know and he knows, behind his sword and goggles.

Whatever is the danger, whatever is the bother, he quite foxily figured out a plot to keep the upper hand.

I'll not take that away. I will assist in any way the growing monster fighter who is figuring out a way to take on the evils of the world.

But I will, for now, always tiptoe back to make sure the little goggles are not squeezing his little sleeping eyeballs.

Heart to Heart

On Quelling Butterflies, and Baby Steps to Prayer

The little red heart is the size of a button. So is its twin, the other half of its whole.

When the sun peeks in my little one's room, when he bounds out of bed and into his school clothes, he'll slip his into his pocket. As his mama will too, with the one of her own. I promised I would.

A heart in your pocket is a very good thing. Especially on the very first day, the very first *long* day of the very first grade, when the time between the morning's goodbye at the schoolhouse door and the zigzag home from the bus stop is wholly untrodden and feels like forever, way past lunch in a lunchroom, and scrambling all over at recess, way past standing in lines and marching through halls, past sitting in chairs and reaching in desks. Way past finding your name on all sorts of supplies, and even a locker you barely know how to begin to use. Way, way past anything you've ever imagined.

A heart in your pocket is a very good thing.

You give it a squeeze when you need to. You give it a squeeze when you're sad. Or wobbly. Or lonesome. You give it a squeeze when you're certain its powers will work like a cell phone, connect you in magical ways, without even dialing. And the heart on the other end of the line will be there, will know that you're calling, really she will.

Because hearts in the pocket are like that.

They connect you.

When you are six and going off in the world, for the very first time really.

Motherprayer

For the very first time when the lumps in your tummy and the ones in your throat are so very big you think they might choke you. Or send you flying to the faraway boys' room, way, way, *way* down the hall, before it's too late.

The need for a heart, the need for a something, became wholly apparent last night in the dark.

That's when hearts are bared. That's when all that is hiding comes out of the shadows. That's when your room and your bed get overly crowded. That's when the things that behave all through the day come haunting. They decide in the night that they want some airtime. They want to romp in your head, stir up a rumpus.

And that's when the feet came. Tiptoeing down the stairs, around the corner, right to my side, that's when the words came too: "Mama, I need to talk to you about something really serious about school."

So, of course, I stopped what I'd thought was important, scooped him onto my lap, and listened.

"I think I'll be homesick."

That was round 1. Before it was ended, we'd talked, reclimbed the stairs, retucked boy into bed, rekissed that curly-haired head.

Then came round 2.

Again, feet shuffling.

This time I was not far from his room. This time the words came in whispers, barely audible whispers there at the top of the stairs, where I promptly sat down.

"I'm nervous about tomorrow. I'm afraid I might vomit."

The child goes straight for the heart. Cuts no corners. Softens no blows.

In a word, he took me right back. Took me back to the weeks, there were two of them, one in kindergarten, one in first grade, when I, too, got so sick, so dehydrated, they twice tossed me in the hospital. I remember it vividly. Remember the little pink puppet they sent me home with. But I remember other things, too, that weren't quite so nice. Things that still give me shudders.

I know what it is to be so afraid, so rumbly inside that you can't hear a word, and the room feels as though it's swirling.

I took my boy by the hand. We had some digging to do.

"We need a heart," I informed him as I led him. As if I knew just how to fix this. As if I were a sorcerer and I held the potion that would cure whatever ailed him. Sometimes even parents play pretend. Because they have to. Because sitting there falling apart would not help. Would not do a thing.

So we pretend that we've all sorts of lotions and potions and balms. We dab cream on a cut, make it feel better. Whip up concoctions to take out the sting. We do voodoo and rain dances, for crying out loud. Whatever it takes to get over the bumps.

The bump last night called for a little red heart. Or a little wee something. Something he could slip in his pocket and know I was there. *Right* there. Not down the street, around the corner, and four blocks south.

So we dug through my top drawer, the one where I stash all my treasures. There was a rock shaped like a heart, a tarnished old ring, a bunny the size of a quarter. And the two red see-through hearts.

We sifted and sorted. I let him decide. I told him how his big brother, too, used to go off in the world "with me in his pocket." Explained how it worked. How you give it a squeeze and you know that I'm there. That I'm thinking. And loving. And waiting. For the end of the day when he'll be home again.

I told him I, too, would have him in my pocket. I, too, would carry a heart. Give it a squeeze. Send a signal. All day, back and forth, little hearts would be flying. Would be defying all logic and sense, and even some science.

But they'd not ever quit. Would not break. Nor run out of batteries. They are forever.

And isn't this a paradigm—a starter kit, a seed pot—for prayer? Isn't this how a child begins to grasp the mystery? How—wordlessly or otherwise—you can reach beyond your frangible self at any hour? How you might not hear a whisper in reply, might not feel the hand of God squeeze tight your fingers or softly lay a palm at the small of your back, but—just as your mama has taught you through the all-day promise to squeeze a red-button heart—you might soon come to understand that God, tender God, is always on patrol, keeping watch, breathing hallowed susurrations to your unsettled soul?

Good thing when you're six, you know things by heart. And you believe, most of all, the things your mama tells you.

Especially at night, especially past bedtime, when all of your insides come burbling right out. When the house has no noise and the moon guides your way down the stairs.

That is the hour that's blessed. That is the hour that mamas and papas and all the people who love you pull out their needles and thread, and even their little red buttons, whatever it takes to stitch you and your heart back together again.

The Gospel of the Pillow

On the Holy Wisdom of the Child

The day had been long, had been wretched, had been draining in that way that day after day of worry can make it.

The task at hand, at least according to the books, was getting the little one into bed. The clock said so. The dark said so. Only the little one seemed to dissent. He seemed wide enough awake for a few innings of baseball.

So I was the one who slid onto the sheets, curled in a ball, and lay there, eyes closed. Just breathing. Feeling the rise and fall of my chest. Hearing my heart. My heart that all day had felt as if it were trudging a mountain. Or cracking in half.

That's when the boy who struggles with words, the ones that get jammed in the lead of his pencil, climbed in beside me and spoke: "Are you hurt? Are you worried? Are you tired?

"You need to sleep," he said, touching my hair.

"Grown-ups," he told me matter-of-factly, "are more important than kids.

"You want your grown-up to stay alive to keep you safe."

He started to put his hands to the back of my nightgown. He made little circles where the angel wings might have started to sprout, back when God was deciding if we'd be the species with wings or without.

He was the putter-to-bed, this long, achy night. It was my little one, with his hands and his words, who woke me from my over-drained stupor. I didn't move, didn't flinch, but I tell you my spine tingled. Had I not wanted to scare him I would have sat suddenly up. His words pierced through to my heart.

I whispered them back, as if a refrain. "You want your grown-up to stay alive to keep you safe."

I realized that was his prayer. Mine too. *Dear God*, I whispered so no one could hear, *give me strength.* The sort of strength I'd needed before. The strength to get up a mountain. To look out from the summit.

Earlier that evening, I'd been in a church listening to a very wise soul. A woman who'd once struggled with polio. She said, and she meant it, "You can survive anything. You have to decide to survive."

I decided then and there that my weary old bones had nowhere to go except to lie by the side of my lastborn. I let his hands' little circles and his words wash over me, fill me, soothe my twittering heart.

I asked him then about grown-ups, about why he thought they might be more important than kids (a point I would argue, if not in inquisitive mode).

"They make your food," was his very first thought, one that came without pause. "They check it out at the store. And they make it, the farmers do.

"They're good for the environment, the garbage people are," he continued.

"They stop people from doing mean things," was the last of his litany.

I lay there absorbing the gospel according to the one whose head shared the pillow. I lay there thinking how God speaks to us, some hours, in the voice of a six-year-old boy.

I lay there feeling the tenderness, feeling the power of his wisdom. I marveled long and hard at the miracle of how the teacher speaks to the student at the hour of absolute need.

I marveled at the clairvoyance of a child. How a child sees through the thick of a heart, through the tangle. How a child, as if a surgeon who works with micro-sized scalpels, can incise right to the core of the matter. Can feed in the words that the heart needs to hear. Can wake up even the sleepy.

I thought, as I reached out and stroked his soft curls, "No, my sweet, the grown-up is the one who desperately, deeply needs the eyes and the voice of the child."

At my house last night, it was the child who was keeping the grown-up so very safe.

Worm Rescue

On Teaching Tenderness

The rains pelted hard all morning. Ruined any notion of lobbing balls out back or sliding into home. Canoeing, maybe, from third to home, but no head-first belly flop onto base. Not without a periscope and flippers.

When it slowed, at last, and came more like the dribble from a cranky faucet that won't quite shut off, the two of us—one of whom had been pouting at the soggy windowsill—decided it was the perfect interlude for the age-old constitutional: the walk, just after the rain.

In fact, I told the little one, as we slid our arms into the yellow rubber sleeves of our water-fighting armor, as he insisted he make the duck umbrella burp and stretch out her wiry ribs, this was a made-to-order meteorological moment for a pair of sidewalk crusaders.

It's nouns like that, I tell you, that prick up a little boy's ears. He looked right at me with that umbrella already doubling as sword. *Crusaders?* I could hear his little brain gears crunching in dismay. *What does she know about crusades?*

"It's worm-rescue weather," I told him, stepping out the door and over the rivulet running east along the stoop. "This is when the worms come out, thinking they'll just grab a little gulp of rain. But then, sometimes, the rains dry up and the poor worms are stranded there on all the sidewalks."

I leapt right in, waited not for him to play along. Or even sign a waiver of intent.

"Here wormy, wormy, wormy," I called, scanning here and there for a waylaid invertebrate, a worm who'd lost its way, a worm, by golly, who'd had far too much to drink and could not slither home. Or just had given in to wormly *je ne sais quoi*. Ennui, perhaps, of the earthworm ilk. Up and called it quits in the middle of a concrete wasteland.

The little one—too young to drop me by the hand and sprint, too old to merely play along—interrupted.

"Hey, Mom, I don't think that's gonna work," he said. "I think that just works for a cat or a dog. But then you have to say their name, the cat's name or the dog's name. Doggy, doggy doesn't work. And wormy, wormy doesn't either."

Oh.

He had a point, but I had little option. No worms I knew had names. Or not that I'd been told. So I kept my eyes to the task. Scanned all the way to the corner. But didn't see a worm, only a stick that I thought—from far away—might have wriggled once or twice but, upon close inspection, didn't.

It was then, faced with sidewalk north or east, that I asked: "Which way has the most worm potential?"

To which he answered, proud with logic: "Why would I know that? I'm not a worm."

Have you noticed that kids these days have surrendered their imaginations? Ah, but then he came through with plain old common sense, imagination's reliable—if not inventive—relation.

"Anyways, Mom, can I tell you something?" he asked, not slowing for an answer. "There's a robin. So, bingo, there must be worms somewhere."

Crouching down, the boy who claimed no insight into worm brainworks began talking to a peachy-breasted bird: "Robin, find a worm for us."

On command, the bird bobbed down its head and came up with a squirmy specimen. The robin, though, failed to cough it up, instead feasting on its sodden insides.

It took three more blocks of worm patrol before, at last, we found a spineless wonder stranded on the walk.

It had inches to go before it made it back to dirt and grass, where it stood a chance of escaping errant tricycles or big flat soles that paid no mind to where they landed.

As I knelt down to teach the tender art of lifting on a stick and plopping the straggler onto the grass, my trusty sidekick kicked in, all right.

"Oh, worm," he started in, "just to tell you, you're disgusting." And then to robin on a limb: "Oh, robin, here's a worm."

It is slow teaching, this curriculum of tenderness toward all things living, and even those that aren't.

As long as they've been watching, the boys I call my own have known their mama to be some sort of creepy-crawler ferry. On a mission from God, perhaps, to let no winged thing, or multilimbed one either, suffer crushing fate or die in a wad of toilet paper.

Why, heck, they tell their friends, she carries ants and flies and even bumblebees out of doors to set them free. In the dead of winter, egad, she lets them loose down in the cellar where it's warm enough for a cold-blooded critter.

And now, in turn, I watch the older one, the much bigger brother, do the same.

The little one, though, is waffling. On the fence about these creatures from the deep and dark side.

But there's hope, I sense.

Stay with me here, as we leave the world of bugs and travel to a new-car showroom.

Just the other night, we found a wee sedan, a shiny black one, to replace the only one my little one had ever known.

When the man in the shiny pinstriped suit spelled out the deal, said in no uncertain terms that we had to turn in the old and not-so-shiny auto, the little one broke into tears that would not stop.

Half an hour later, the tears still poured. Not even lemonade and kisses squelched the flow. Not even big-screen TV, with baseball nearly big as life, squawking in the little room where they make you dawdle while they write up all the zeroes.

His face all red and splotchy, the worm-resistor whispered in my ear: "Can I go give the car a kiss goodbye?"

And so, by the hand I took the boy I'm teaching to be full of heart. We walked into the greasy place marked Service, where they stripped the trusty car of its old plates and emptied out its trunk, with nowhere near the honor, by the way, that it deserved.

My little one leaned on the hood, blessed the car with a tender kiss, then stretched his arms as far as he could reach around the grille. He laid his cheek onto the hood. And squeezed with all his might.

He might not have mastered the fat and squirmy earthworm, but he showed the other night that there's quite a heart inside that little chest.

Next time it rains, we'll try again to beat the robins and rescue stranded nameless creatures who have no legs to get them where they're headed.

Four Score and So Many Tears

On Hearing, Really Hearing, the Deep-Down Script of a Child's Heart

It wasn't on our way. But we steered there anyway.

A red-lined triangle on the road map was all it took. That and what turned into a few hours' drive through the mountains, in the rain, with no shoulder to the right, and big trucks barreling by on the left.

There was that boy in the backseat, after all, the boy who'd learned all the words, who'd traced the story of the president who'd ended slavery, and who somehow had decided that to settle his own hard-thumping heart, he'd needed to slip the soles of his shoes into the very same spot on the crest of the hill where the words were first declaimed. In the midst of the half-circles of square white stones, unmarked soldiers' graves, state-by-state in the most somber of roll calls.

It was the Gettysburg Address, three short paragraphs really, that he'd learned at school, read out loud in assembly, recited one night at dinner, delightfully reading "deducted" instead of "dedicated" each time he came to that particular mix of Ds and Cs and Ts that, quite honestly, is so indistinguishable to an orator of a mere seven years.

And so, since we were driving to Washington anyway, he figured, why not swing up into Pennsylvania, that bread-loaf-shaped chunk in the jigsaw puzzle, not far from the DC triangle, and drive to the little town where the great speech was etched into the national memory.

It wasn't enough, on that chilly afternoon, to merely drive through the town, stand in some parking lot marked Visitor Center, and rip out the sheet with the words.

Oh, no.

We stopped for a map and directions. We wiggled our way through fields once soaked in blood. We parked near the crest of a hill, walked past long stone fences, crossed a country road, and walked and walked until we couldn't get closer to where Mr. Lincoln's shoes must have fallen, stood firm against the hard, cold soils that had seen and heard too much, blest the mound where soldiers at last were laid to rest and peace and the broadcloth of history.

The little boy, one who most of the time spouts numbers and news about ball fields and the players who play there, somehow had been trans-fixed by these words and this speech and this spot on the map.

There was no steering him elsewhere. No approximation of history.

He'd decided it had to be just as it was. Had to be he reading the words out loud, to the cold winds and the three grown-ups (his big brother, after all, is nearly a grown-up) who love him so very much, who stood somewhat astonished at this whole insistence on honoring history.

He'd carried a parchment, written in script, signed "Abraham Lincoln, November 19, 1863," but he couldn't make out the nineteenth-century swirls and dips and swoops of soot-black ink.

So, when we'd stopped for the map, he'd handily gotten the words typed out, more to his liking, more like the pages of books he now reads by the hour, this boy who not long ago struggled with words in any old form.

So there we were at the top of the hill, just in front of the great marble monument, with the plaque marking the spot.

The boy, seven and change, settled in, maybe as Lincoln had, pulled the words from his pocket, unfolded the ridges, and began.

"Four score," he started, of course. And then carried on. The words coming in that familiar cadence and rhythm we all know, all of us who in some schoolroom somewhere pored over the Civil War pages, tried our hand at memorizing, maybe for the first time, with this particular passage.

Somewhere, though, near the part where Lincoln wrote that "we can not dedicate, we can not consecrate, we can not hallow this ground," the words slowed to nearly a halt.

We looked in, each of us, zeroed our eyes on his face, trying to read the root of the slowed-down reading.

Only then, as the next few words sputtered, did I see what I thought looked like a tear. And then another and another.

He was crying and reading, the boy who would not let the tears stop the cadence, the moment, not until the end when we all crushed him, a tangle of arms, cheeks, tears.

"Sweetheart, what is it?" I asked, not sure if it was the hard words that had netted his courage, swallowed his sense of the moment, or whether it was the sad truth of the story, the soldiers buried in half moons and rows all around.

"It's the soldiers," he managed to choke out, before burying his face in my sleeve.

We all stood in this knot for a minute or two. I knew that I, for one, was etching the moment into my mind, into my picture of this boy who I'd birthed, this boy who not often was thought of as the one with his pulse in sync with the poetry and prayer of a world marred by bloodshed and tombstones.

Sometimes on a cold afternoon, at the crest of history, you discover the script that you've inked in your head, the script of your own child, it's not what you thought it was.

His is a soul, you suddenly see, with volumes that reach back and forth in time, that catch the cadence of grief from another era and bring it to life. Put breath to its torment and loss, stir afresh its unending sting.

And you stand there, wiping back tears, his and your own. And all of a sudden you understand a whole new chapter has been written; a whole new glimpse of the soul, revealed.

One you will never forget.

A Season for Soooooo Sorry

On Forgiveness

It was more or less the usual bumbling that comes when a boy and a backpack are tumbled together. Things that are supposed to get stuffed inside, aren't. Where they go, nobody knows.

Only thing was, last eve the clock chimed eight as we discovered the spelling list was nowhere to be had. Which led to the discovery that the whole dang homework folder was missing in action. Which led to the theorem, posited by young boy, that since none of the above was anywhere in this old house, it must be somewhere in the depths of his school desk. Without prompting, he confessed: "It's pretty messy, I probably couldn't find it."

Which led to the low, moaning rumble that sometimes comes from a motherly creature when she is trying to decide whether to yank out a clump of her own hair or grab the car keys and hope against hope that one of the nice janitors will wander with mop and bucket past the schoolhouse door just as she and her little one are banging away on the glass.

Not willing to spare any more of my curly pewter locks, we went with the option with keys. Flew through the door, into the wagon, and sputtered along until we got to the nearly dark school.

From the start, at least one of us knew deep inside that this was an exercise in utter futility. But we banged on the glass anyway. It makes for a loud impression when hoping to teach that one oughtn't race out the school door without packing essentials.

Alas, no janitor. No mop and no bucket. Just us banging and hoping.

Soon watching hope whirl down the drain and turning at last back toward the curb and the futile-mobile.

Once home, I told the little one to sit down with a pencil and try as hard as he could to remember the twenty-two words on the list. Or at least four or five.

While he got to work with the pencil, I sat down to dash off a note to the teacher. Explaining why the quiz on those words, the one on the morrow, might be a bust.

That's when a lined sheet of notebook paper came swooshing under the door. I looked down and saw only two words, under the heading "MY Words."

"Is that all you could think of?" I called to the invisible someone who had shoved it under the door.

"Look at it," the invisible someone called back.

"Is that all you could remember?" I said again, frustration clutching my throat.

"Look at it," said Mr. Invisible.

And so I did. I picked up the page, and there on the back was a lopsided heart. And another one tucked in a sentence up at the top: "I (heart) you."

His rumply letters continued: "I am soooooo sorry I'll make you brekfast and coffe love Ted"

Be still my lopsided heart.

Be still my heart that couldn't care more for the two extraordinary spellings there in the note.

Through tears, I leapt up from my chair. Chased that irresistible speller straight up the stairs, where I grabbed him and kissed him until he melted to giggles.

Then I stood there melting myself.

That he would leap straight to "sorry," rather than pout or huff and puff about how it was only some words, lined up in rows.

That he would hightail it straight through repent and onto repair—"I'll make you brekfast and coffe."

All because of some runaway spelling words...

The child had grasped, without pausing for punctuation, without worry for vowels in absentia, the heart and the soul of atonement, of Yom Kippur, really, that somber string of breast-beating moments that is launched, according to the Hebrew calendar that is ours as much as the Gregorian keeper of days, at sundown tonight.

It is all about actively mending the brokenness. Not just whispers of hollow apology, but picking up thread and stitching sanctified wholeness. Weave and reweave.

Just yesterday I was talking to a wise and wonderful rabbi. We were talking about *teshuva*, the Jewish principle of repentance—repent and repair—the centerpiece of these Days of Awe, of the Day of Atonement.

"I have sinned, and for this I am heartily sorry."

The words of the Prayer of Contrition of my little-girl days.

Catholic or Jewish, Jewish or Catholic—is it not all a great swirl, a soup of humble I've-wronged-and-I'll-right-it?

And it came skittering in through the crack beneath my door last night, the wise little confessor with the wobbly printing and the words that couldn't have been cobbled together in more heart-melting fashion.

Brekfast and coffe and sorry and love.

And isn't this some sweet season of awe, when the children among us can teach as profoundly as all of the rabbis? When the scribbled words on a half-crinkled page of notebook paper can speak to us as loudly as the words of the great books of our ancient traditions?

"I am soooooo sorry I'll make you brekfast and coffe"

Oh, my most blessed child, you've taken my breath straight from my lungs, from my heart, from my whole.

We thought it was spelling words we were missing last night; in fact, we found deepest religion, a subject often best taught by the youngest and wisest among us.

The ones whose hearts are, still, tethered to heaven.

From the Cookery Files...

When a pouf of billowy sweetness is called for, when you're inclined to pull from the oven a golden-domed cloud of the original comfort foodstuffs: bread + milk + sugar + eggs. Isn't that the nursery maid's tried and true prescription, the one sure cure for whenever life pummels in hard-to-take blows?

Elixir Pudding

Excuse me while we interrupt our regularly scheduled programming to bring you the following emergency announcement: you must, I mean must, go directly to where you keep your bread that is old, that is galloping swiftly toward stale.

You must grab it before it goes straight down the hill. Now rip it in bits. Big bits are fine, if that's the bit of your choosing. Little bits work as well. As do bits somewhere in the middle.

We are en route to bread pudding, that soft, mushy pillow of succor, the one with the cinnamon-sugary crust, providing just the right edge to your puff. The pudding of which one ample spoonful turns us all back into tots.

You'll be aswirl, at the very first taste, in visions of nurseries and prams and old English nannies, with considerable bosoms, leading you on with a ladle. Or, you'll simply swallow and hum.

The reason we're rushing is this: the recipe I concocted, with a little help from Mark Bittman, he who teaches us how to cook *everything*, seems to have cast a sort of spell. I think it's a pudding possessed.

So much so, I must proselytize, attempt to persuade you. My little one, who spooned it up for dessert, then again before bedtime, and then, not twelve hours later, once more for breakfast, looked at me dreamy-eyed from under his curls and inquired: "Will you make it for Christmas?"

And the firstborn, so inspired was he, he sent me a love note (*yes*, a pudding-y love note): "The pudding was great. I needed it today. Life wouldn't be worth living without such a home to come to. I really mean it. Love, love, love."

What I want to know is, who mixed the elixir in with the eggs and the butter and bread-on-the-verge-of-bread-crumbing?

I saw no one there in the kitchen, but some invisible hooligan must have been fooling with me and my bread bits. What happened is this: there I was, minding my start-of-week business, when suddenly I heard a whisper from there in the corner, from the basket where tired old bread sits before dying.

"Come, come," it called. I swear that it did.

And before I knew it, I was off to the bookshelf, hauling down my old friend Mr. Bittman.[4] Right there, on page 662 of his tome, bread pudding in three easy steps. So I followed instructions, then I vamped—made it *my* elixir bread pudding. I grated some apple into my pudding. I tossed in whole fistfuls of raisins. And I dusted the top with a bumper crop of cinnamon and vanilla-infused sugar.

And the results, as I mentioned, were utterly stunning. Never before seen.

To come up with something that had my boys so starry-eyed, well, that is a day to press to the heart. May the coos and the star-dazzled eyes be many at your house.

Elixir Bread Pudding

Provenance: Mark Bittman's How to Cook Everything *+ imagination, my own*

Yield: 1 batch, or 6 servings

3 cups milk
4 tablespoons unsalted butter, plus some for greasing the pan
1½ teaspoons cinnamon, divided
½ cup plus 1 tablespoon sugar, divided (I make a habit of
    burying a vanilla pod in my sugar canister, so my white
    sugar is always infused with Tahitian vanilla notes)
¼ teaspoon salt
Best day-old bread you can find (Mr. Bittman calls for 8 slices;
    I reached for the remains of a loaf of *challah*, the braided
    egg bread we bring to the table for every Shabbat)

3 eggs
I apple, grated
I or 2 fistfuls raisins, cranberries, or your choice from the
     dried-fruits department

Preheat oven to 350 degrees Fahrenheit. Over low heat in a saucepan, warm milk, butter, I teaspoon cinnamon, ½ cup sugar, and
salt, just until butter melts. Meanwhile, butter a I½-quart baking
dish or 8-inch square pan. Cut and tear bread into bite-size bits.

Place bread in baking dish. Pour hot, buttery milk over it.
Sigh as you pour. Let milk sit for a bit, occasionally dunking any
recalcitrant bits not willing to tread milk. Beat the eggs and stir
into bread mixture. Add I cup grated, drained apple and hand-
ful of raisins. Mix remaining cinnamon and sugar, and sprinkle
over the top. Set the baking dish into a larger baking pan and
pour hot water into the pan to within an inch of the top of the
dish. (You're indulging your pudding-filled dish in an oven-y
steam bath.)

Bake 45 minutes to I hour, or until a thin-bladed knife
comes clean from the center; center should be just a bit wobbly.
Run under the broiler for about 30 seconds to get that yummy
golden-brown crust. Serve warm or cold. With whipped cream.
Keeps well for two days covered in the refrigerator, but I don't
think it'll stick around even half that long. It never lingers at
our house.

Brooding: Keeping Close Watch, Savoring All the While

Sleeping sentries: Even when apparently asleep, birds open their eyes and peek around. Peeking is limited to the phase of sleep referred to as dozing or "quiet sleep." During the remaining "active-sleep" portion of slumber, birds' eyes remain shut. Animal behaviorist Dennis Lendrem surveyed flocks of dozing ducks until the patterns of peeking could be discerned. Lendrem found that in the ducks peeking typically occurred about once every two to six seconds.[1]

—*The Birder's Handbook: A Field Guide to the Natural History of North American Birds*

Not Too Big

On the Slipping Away of Something You've Loved

*A*ny day now, it'll evaporate.

I'll look out the window and not see the little boy bundled in snow suit and puffy snow pants, the one too little, at six, to know it's quite little-boyish to pull up that hood, pull it so tight that only his little-boy cheeks, all rosy and round, poke out from the layers of puff upon puff. I won't see, anymore, how he kicks that one chunk of snow all the way home, from bus stop to house, a ten-minute meander that has him winding and spinning and kicking and scooping and, yes, *ykkh*, licking that snow.

Any day now, I won't walk in his room to kiss him awake, only to find at the foot of his bed an old cardboard box he's made into a house for his little stuffed rabbits, the twosome he's tucked into bed, maybe read them by flashlight a story, whispered their prayers, then kissed them goodnight.

Any day now, he won't fit on my hip, that perch of old bone that was built, I'm convinced, to hold up a child in tears, or in heartache, or, every once in a while, in deep cuddling mode.

Any day now, his legs will get longer, his words will get less of that little-boy lisp. And the occasional lapse into pure make-believe will go *poof*, will vanish overnight.

There won't be a bear with a name. We won't set a place at the table for that wild-haired lion named Leo (a cat who insists, by the way, on Rice Chex topped with bananas, more milk, please; a diet eerily close to the one thing his trainer could eat—and does—morning, noon, and most every night).

Any day now, he'll be all gone, my sweet little boy.

He'll be replaced by a model less likely, I'm supposing, to give me a rub on my back for no reason besides the fact that he still loves the feel of my skin. He won't want to climb in my bed and play twenty questions on Saturday mornings. And I doubt he'll hand me the phone and ask me to dial because all the numbers just mix him all up.

So, right now, and right here, I have every intention of cupping it all in the palm of my hand. Like sweet and cool waters, there at the edge of the stream on a day that's unbearably dry.

I'll suck it all up, every last drop, before it slithers away, slips through my fingers and back to the stream, where it rushes away.

I won't get it again. This water comes once, comes in a rush that at first feels too much, too hard to swallow, even in gulps. But then, as it goes, as it trickles away, down your wrists, down your arms, back to the stream, you feel, already, the parch in your throat.

Of late, the pangs come often, come hard. I miss him already. I long for these days, and they're not even gone yet.

It's a trick of the brain, a trick of the heart. And it's not just a trick for the mamas among us. All of us, every one, we know what it is to miss someone we love before they're not here anymore.

It's the thing, is it not, that churns deep in our souls, propels us to love and love deeper. To cherish. To know, in our blood, with the swirls of our fingertips even, that what's in our midst is sacred, is holy, is never forever.

And so, I go through my day with one extra eye. It's trained on the child growing before me. I reach out and grab when the moments are sweet, and then all the sweeter.

The boy with the bear. The boy who climbs, still, on my lap. Takes my hand in a crowd, squeezes it tight. The boy who calls out my name in the night and awakes curled in a ball in the morning, all flannel and cowboy pajamas, and rosy and toasty, and playing like a possum.

It is a hard thing in this world to know how to ready a child for all that awaits, a planet of wars and digital overload. A world where too many children are bounding toward grown-up, skipping right over the parts that teach them tender is golden, is good, is—in my book—truly essential.

So I stick with the basics, with what I know best, and what I believe with all of my whole. And I let it all play in the slowest of slo-mo.

I relish the old cardboard box and the chance to tuck a bunny into bed. I aim for the winding way home. And a sweet little boy in no hurry to harden.

I'll savor each drop of each day. And know, soon enough, I'll be ever so thirsty. And my sweet little boy will be big. Too big for my hip. But never, my heart. Which grows right along with him.

Cinnamon Toast & Pear Slices: Gathering Grace Wherever It Falls

On Soaking Up Joy, Pure and Simple

These might be called the sawdust days—dry and rough and shaved into crumbles.

Some nights I fall into bed, thinking, hoping, praying maybe my tossings and turnings, the brackets in between sleep, will clear out my head and my heart and my soul.

But then I wake up in the morning, flop my feet on the floor, feel the twinge up my leg. And the one that gnaws at my heart. The one that weighs me down.

Oh, it's all sorts of somethings. The news from the box by the side of the bed, the one I ought to change, maybe, to Mozart instead of the global markets' collapse. Then there's the news that comes folded on paper, the paper that's brought me my paycheck all these years, and the love of my life, and both our boys; our double bylines, we call them. Brought me a lifetime's adventures, too. And the chance to soak up the stories of everyday saints and unsinkable sinners. But these days, it's all turned on its head—layoffs and buyouts are everyday news in the newsroom; so, too, the slashing of newsprint and stories. It's all making me dizzy.

So it is that I walk through these hours, sometimes aching and often-times wincing. I swallow back tears more often than anyone knows.

And I gather up grace, wherever it falls.

I've been through these kinds of days before. I've learned what it takes. The one sure holy equation.

It's grace gathering, pure and simple.

And its holiest spark is how it comes cloaked in the plainest of cloth. Doesn't come at you blinking and beeping and flashing bright lights. You just lay down a footstep and find that you've entered compartments of grace.

Just today it came in cinnamon toast, studded with raisins, slathered with butter and drifted with mounds of cinnamon sugar. That toast shared the plate with a pear, sliced and juicy and waiting. For someone.

My little one, the one who brings me grace by the gallon these days, he was due to bound in the door any minute. I, too, had just stumbled in, as a matter of fact. Day before, I'd plain missed the after-school hour, typing away at my faraway desk, the one in the newsroom downtown.

I could've skipped right over this moment, too, this chance, this grace in the wings. Could have mad-dashed back to my desk here at home. Back to the work that's never quite done.

But then, without folderol, without the trill of a drum, those scant few minutes—the ones when the backpack is shed and the stories spill fiercely—they invited me in.

Come, come, they whispered. *Partake.* Take a moment, lift this up from this everyday altar. Break bread. Then, while you're at it, the moments insisted, take it and toast it. Lay it out where he'll see it, where he'll know in an instant: she was waiting for me. My mama, she knows how to feed me.

And so, grace descended on us, wrapped us, tight in the blanket of side-by-side comfort.

Grace is balm for the soul. It feeds us in places that growl with unworldly hunger. It moistens the parts that are parched.

Grace is the prayer beads we string in a row. The rosary of life lived at attention. It's the layer of soul tied to Divine.

And it comes unannounced most every time.

It comes, yes, in cinnamon toast. It comes, too, in the molasses light of October, the way it catches on the last dying petal of the black-eyed Susan I stubbornly keep in the vase on the sill.

Motherprayer

It comes in the moon playing peekaboo behind the whipped-cream swirls of the clouds in the night sky, a frolic so wholly delicious you stop on your way to dump out the trash, and next thing you know you're humming along with all of the stirrings that come from the boughs and the bushes—a rhapsody you wouldn't have heard, wouldn't have taken in gulps, but for the something called grace that slowed you and held you. And seeped in through the cracks.

It comes, grace does, like the brush of the great palm of God, there on your brow.

Be filled, it urges. *Take heart*, it commands.

The world is more than you know, more than you see. There is, at work every hour, a layer of beauty and truth and infinite wisdom.

Its name is grace.

Gather it greedily. It's there for the hungry, the thirsty, the aching.

It's there for the ones who believe. And it's there for the ones who barely remember.

The Hours That Matter the Most

On Listening

As I sift through the grains of my week, of my year, of my long stretch of motherhood, I've come to know that the grains I hold a bit longer, the grains I hold up to the light, are the fine, simple hours that come, often, right after school, or tucked into tight spots at the oddest of times.

When the boys I love are bothered, are troubled, are weighed down with the grit of the day.

When suddenly the chairs at the table are pulled. Bottoms splot onto cane-woven seats. When teacups are cradled in palms. When oranges are peeled, piled in sections.

When the talking begins.

Of all the scores of things I might do in a week, in a lifetime, nothing perhaps matches the wholeness of those holy hours.

The boys I love are sifting through their own hearts, laying their troubles at my chest, at my heart. They are trusting not my mouth but my ears.

Just listen, you can hear them hoping.

Just hear all my words, spoken and not.

Just listening alone will heal, will soothe, go a long way toward fixing.

When days are bad, when hours are bumpy, most of the time we aren't looking for quick cures or Band-Aids. All we want, really, is someone to sop up the hurt. To listen to worries.

All we want, often, are eyes that look deep, look gently. Eyes that listen. Not words that cut off. Not words that dismiss.

Just hear me, you can hear the hearts saying. If you listen. Just listen.

And so, unscripted, unplanned, the scene plays over and over. One minute we're there at the sink, I might be chopping or rinsing, a child is circling the kitchen. The talking begins.

The kettle is cranked. The tea bags and cups pulled from the cupboards. Teakettle whistles. Stories are spilling.

I walk to the table, two teacups in hand. Chairs are pulled out. Each of us sits. I lean in, my chest pressed against the edge of the table, tilting toward the one who is talking.

The quieter I sit, the more wholly I take in the words, the deeper the place from which the words come.

It's a curious algebra, the one of the heart.

On the surface, perhaps, it appears to be one-way. But in fact, the art of listening is a most active one. You take in, you sift, you turn each morsel of thought, you examine, allow the questions to rise. But you wait. You hold your questions off to the side, in a queue, on hold. Patiently waiting their turn.

When it's time, when the pause comes, you reel out the questions, one, or maybe a string. You sit and you wait.

A question, constructed with care, unspooled on the river of talk, is one that sinks deep, one that says, *I am with you in thought. We are in this together. Our heads and our hearts entwined, teamed up. You're not alone. I wonder, too.*

No solution need come. No answers, plucked from the current.

In fact, it might not be until later that night, or a week or a year down the road, when the one you talked to realizes that all those hours, strung on a line that never breaks, have woven themselves into a cord that connects. A life-string that keeps you from drowning, from sloshing alone in the deep.

It's what you hold on to, with your ears and your heart wide open and your mouth rather hushed.

You remember how deeply you prayed that someone would listen.

You cradle that cup till the sides grow cold, till the sun sets, and the clock inches along.

You know when it's time for homework to start, for dinner to simmer along in the pots.

But in that holy interlude when one heart's ache is offered up, received by another, the weight shared, burden lifted, those are the hours that matter the most.

Those are the hours that answer our prayers.

The ones we've prayed all our lives.

The Things That Moms Just Know

On the Power of Paying Attention

The boy with his spoon in the loops mumbled something this morning that sounded as though a family of mmm's had gone out to the carnival, climbed onto the bumper car ride, and rumbled their way through the course.

"Mmm, mm m mm mmmm mmm mm?"

"Oh," said I, "you want some orange juice?"

He nodded, then swallowed.

Not thinking another thing of it, I opened the fridge, reached for the carton and poured.

He, though, looked up from the page where the sports scores are duly recorded. He had that curious look in his eyes.

That's when he did what he so often does: he broke open the ordinary, caused me to stop in my tracks, to pause, to ponder, to pay closer attention.

He said, simply and not simply at all: "I have a question. What are some of the most interesting things that moms just know?"

He pitched the question as if moms were a species unto their own. As if he were at the zoo, peering in from the far side of the bars, and I were one of the slow, meandering mammals, one of those big, furry cats, perhaps, pacing purposefully back and forth in my concrete-slabbed cube, looking out at the crowd, plotting somehow, as I always imagine they do, those poor cats, how to break out of that measly four-walled existence.

My little one, the one with the loops back in his spoon, continued with his morning query: "I mumbled, but you knew exactly what I meant," he explained of the motherly feat that had captured his attention.

"What are some of the really abstract things that you know? The really abstract things that you know about me?"

Ah, yes, the mother, *mater omnes sciens*, mother all knowing, as the Latin scholar would say.

Apparently, to the sweet child, it appears that without trying I mysteriously peer deep into his cerebrum and divine all sorts of nifty things. Say that it's breakfast time, he's been snoring all night in a stuffy little chamber of a room, and he's developed a thirst for the drink he downs each and every morning, give or take the mornings when something more tempting—say, pineapple juice—is in the fridge. He wants me to pour, voilà, a shallow glass of OJ.

To the child, apparently, this appears a motherly trick of pure prestidigitation.

The child, apparently, has no clue that we live and breathe, some of us, to map out the swath of his or her landscape. Said child has no clue that as he shovels pasta tubes into his mouth, we are studying his sweet little face, reading between lines, on patrol at all times for sparks that might be smoldering there in the forest. Or that we are searching, as he rolls through the door after a long day of school, for the slightest telltale flinch, the mere suggestion of a clue that this was a bad day, and we are here, all but tied up in apron strings, the living, breathing emotional-rescue machine.

The child, apparently, has no clue that his entire life long we have been listening, listening intently. We have felt the piercing upon impact of certain words as they simultaneously hit our eardrums and zing straight to our hearts. They have no clue that we have powers of instant memorization, that we tumble some lines, the occasional shard of a word or words, over and over and over in our minds that don't cease, don't know from the pause button.

And thus, whereas we think nothing of reaching for the drink that he drinks breakfast after breakfast, or smearing the same old peanut butter onto the bread that he happens to love more than any, there stands a chance, a slim chance, that the child on rare occasions looks up from his daily existence and catches a glimmer of the miracle that is having someone who loves you, someone who knows you so intently, so deeply, that she is able—without vowels interrupting the string of consonant sounds—to decipher just what it is he desires.

And, without his even saying a word sometimes, she is able to tiptoe into his bedroom at night, on just the right night, and she knows to slip under the sheets, right beside him, and start making those circles on his forehead, the ones that he loves, the ones that make him let down his shoulders, his worries, after a long hard day. And she knows, without his saying a word, just when he needs her to ask, "So how was your day, sweetie?" because she might have asked that question a dozen times already, but it's at bedtime, it's there in the dark, when the words serve to uncork the deep heart of the matter.

Mamas know those things.

They do if they are listening, if they are paying attention. If their own hearts are still enough, if they've spent years deep at work practicing the art of those things that mamas do and know and say and understand and feel through and through.

That's how mamas acquire what to a little boy spooning loops might seem like a list of abstractions. Like how a mama knows by the way a boy bites at his lip that he's just a little bit nervous, or that when he hops a certain way on the ball field it means he is quietly proud of that ball he just caught tight in his mitt, or how she knows—not because it's abstract so much as highly particular—that he likes his cinnamon sugar sprinkled right up to the edge of the buttered toast, and he doesn't like the butter in unmelted lumps, thank you.

Because, in the end, mothering is all about the particulars.

Mothering, at its best, is the art of paying pure attention.

Of knowing, for a good long spell of years anyway, the unspoken land-scape of the unfolding child. Because, after all, we start out this adventure from the very beginning, from before the words come. So we've had years of filling in blanks, from reading the particular shrillness of a cry, from feeling how the little one kicks his legs against the wall of our womb, and later on watching how he does the same on the stretched-out blanket.

I like to think it's my job to be a high-sensory detector. To discern the interior dialogue, the one of his heart, before he's learned the words to put to that script. If I know to ask the right question, if I can lay out the word choice, the possible phrase, then he can begin to pluck from the choices. He can begin to gain fluency in honoring all the feelings that bottle up inside. I can be his guide in the language of self-expression.

And I can be the one who knows that first thing in the morning, when he needs to race to the bus, a mouthful of OJ is just the drink to sweeten, to douse, his dry little throat.

That's no miracle to me. But it is to him. Isn't that the miracle?

And those are just some of the things that mamas just know....

Sacramental Supper

On Holy Communion at the Kitchen Table

*I*t came over me as if I'd been out on a splintering raft in the middle of swallowing seas, as if for days and days I'd not seen dry shore. Nor steady mooring to cling to. But there, not far out of my reach, rose a sea-battered timber anchored in the sandy bottom. The end post of a barnacle-crusted dock I couldn't quite make out, and it came out of nowhere.

Looked like hope to me.

So I reached for it. Reached into the meat bin at the bottom of the fridge. Hauled out the pack of butchered steer. Then I hoisted the cast-iron pot, the one so hefty it could break a toe. A pack of toes. I glopped in a spill of oil, olive oil slick across the now-sizzling surface. And in plopped the cubes of beef. I browned and hummed. That's what cooking on a Thursday morning does.

I was burrowing into the holiness, the sacrament of middle-of-the-week, because-they-need-it, because-we-all-need-it supper. It would be ladled at long day's end, when, for a moment, hands would be clasped, prayers raised, then forks. And a certain emptiness, filled.

That's the mystery and alchemy of all-day puttering at the cookstove. It's the only thing some days, some weeks, that beelines to the crannies in our heart where words can't go. That seeps into hollows hungry for so very much.

Since this was sacramental, after all, I set the altar while beef cubes sizzled: old, chipped Blue Willow plates, ratty napkins that could use a spin through the sewing machine. Cobalt glasses, ones that all day long catch the light, spill streams of celestial blue across the old maple planks of the handed-down kitchen table, the one that still wears the imprint of third-grade homework from 1965 (or so I calculate, judging by the particular child's scrawl and the certain words pressed into the wood).

Sacramentum, the Latin dictionary tells us, means "sign of the sacred."[2] Is it sacrilegious, then, to call a plain old supper, one that simmered on the back burner all day long, one thought through, from spattered sheaf of follow-along instructions clear through to pop-from-a-tube biscuits, is it sacrilegious to call a lump of root vegetables and beef, ones swimming all day long in thyme and bay leaf, crushed tomatoes with a splash of red wine vinegar, is it sacrilegious to call it sacramental?

I think not.

To serve up what amounts to depths of heart, to say in mashed potatoes and Irish butter, "I love you dearly, and I'm so sorry I've been distracted. So sorry I've been heating up old soup, chicken pot pie from a box." To say, with store-bought pumpkin pie, under a swirl of canned whipped cream (I splurged on the one that shouted, "Extra Creamy!"): "Forgive me for making it seem like something else might have been more top-of-the-to-do-list than carving out the blessed half hour (let's not be greedy here) when we all sit down and savor pay-attention cooking. And each other."

Because, really, I think we can taste the difference. Oh, umami is umami. And sweet is sweet. But don't the hours of stirring, of simmering, of thinking something through—not whipping it off in the last ten minutes before the hunger sirens screech—doesn't it all find its way deep down into the deliciousness that doesn't come through shortcut piled atop shortcut?

Yesterday, the day was afghan autumnal, all gray and fuzzy, the sort of day when you hunker inside, when the cookstove yodels to you. When the burners itch to be cranked. And the bins of rutabaga and turnip and parsnip—all those underground offerings that soak up what the earth's deep, dark soil has to share—they beg for vegetable peeler and chopping block and long hours surrendering to flame.

It was the sort of day-after-hubbub when quiet invited me in for a long, slow visit. Nothing rushed about the day. A day to breathe deep, breathe slow. To fill my lungs with quiet prayers, the prayers of lavishing love on the ones so dear to me, the ones who deserve nothing less than the very best dinner I could chop and stir and taste-test along the way. And while I'm at it, why not take it up a zany notch? Just because there's never enough oomph in an ordinary day. And what day, really, deserves to be plain old ordinary?

By suppertime, when the tableau beyond the panes of glass had gone inky black, when the glow of the kitchen lamp spilled gold across the table, the vapors that rose from the big, red smash-your-toes cook pot, the vapors that trespassed out of the oven crept up the stairs to where homework was being done.

Before I'd said a word, the stovetop's incense was deep at work. The house was filled with something surely holy, for what else can you call it when you claim a whole long day to aim for higher?

To say in smell and taste and temperature and touch what words alone just might not say: *You are worth it to me to spend a whole day cooking just for you. I've not lost sight of my holiest calling, to carve out a hallowed space here in this place of walls and windows and creaky floors and solid roof, to be the one reliable source of all that's good, that's edifying. To fill you with warm spoonfuls—as much as you want, there's plenty here. And I've made it beautiful because you are, because beauty speaks to the deep-down whole of us. And you so richly deserve every morsel I can muster.*

The day was chilly brisk. I did what I could to make the kitchen glow, the holy light of heaven here on earth. And to fill those who came to the chairs at long day's end.

Far as I can tell, that's a sacrament, a sign of the sacred. With a fat splat of butter drooling off the plate.

From the Cookery Files...

When a slow stir at the cookstove is the meditation you're after, and peeling and chopping and mashing entice, offering backbeat to your kitchen incantation. When you're hungry for take-it-up-a-notch feasting, and especially when there's a chill in the day, and you're out to blanket the ones you love with a bubbling pot that, more than anything, warms the soul.

Beef Stew Matters

A confession: for days now I've been considering the fine points of stew. I've pondered the layering of flavorful notes. Ruminated over anchovies. Weighed root vegetables. Detailed the pluses of rutabaga, countered with low points of turnip. I've dwelled on umami, that quixotic "fifth taste" we're all after.

At last, I've settled on a road map. Any hour now, I'll be cranking the flame, putting chunks of beef to iron-hot scald of my three-thousand-pound cook pot. It's what you do when you want a fine stew.

Because a wintry stew, served to a hungry tableau, is the *raison d'être* of the season of ice and blustery winds and bone-chilling temps that makes us ponder the wisdom of bears who pack it all up and go under cover from, say, the Thanksgiving feast till the rising of Easter.

I am filling my table with people I love, and a few whom I only scantily know. I am, after all, a believer in the power of putting ideas to the world, and the best place I know for birthing fine thought, for bridging frames of reference, is the dinner table. The way I see it, the dinner table is merely the classroom, the seminar chamber, set with knives, forks, and a battalion of glassware.

And, if you want to bring together great stews of ideas, of stories, of wisdom, of light, you need to stoke the flame with the richest, most sublime assemblage of feast and drink and, yes, a setting or two—or six—from the old-plate collection.

It's why I've been turning to my panel of master teachers, all lined up on the shelves of my kitchen—and a few who walk and talk and dispense real-life secrets. It's why I'm sidling up to David Tanis, a generous-hearted cook (formerly of Chez Panisse and a regular in the *New York Times*) endowed with a down-to-earth soul who finds perfection in a simple soft-boiled egg and who writes that the peeling of carrots and onions for a simple stew "can be meditative."

It's not about wow-ing. It's about allowing the feast to speak for the part of my heart and soul that breathes beyond words.

The equation I'm after is one that's infused with humility, yet banks on the notion that dolloping grace and deliciousness—both in measures sublime—is bound to spiral the talk a notch or two and kindle the room with a shared sense of the sacred: this table matters, what unfolds here is sacramental; and, as the one who's done the gathering, I've infused it with the very best I could muster.

*My Secret
Ingredient
Beef Stew*

Provenance: Ree Drummond, Pioneer Woman *blog* + *Amanda Hesser,*
Food52 *blog* + *David Tanis,* the New York Times

Yield: 8 servings

2 tablespoons olive oil
3 pounds beef stew meat (chuck roast, cubed)
salt and pepper
1 whole medium onion, diced
2 leeks, sliced
7 cloves garlic, minced
2 carrots, peeled and chopped
1 (8-ounce) package cremini (or baby bella) mushrooms
6 ounces tomato paste
2 anchovies
½-ounce packet dried porcini mushrooms*

½ cup red wine vinegar
I cup canned whole tomatoes with juice (or I can)
4 cups low-sodium beef broth, more if needed for thinning
I½ teaspoons salt
2 bay leaves
¾ teaspoon dried thyme
2 whole carrots, peeled and diced
I whole turnip, peeled and diced
½ rutabaga, peeled and diced
I parsnip, peeled and diced
I cup pearl onions (I use frozen)
⅓ cup fresh parsley, minced

* An optional splurge. Or if, like me, you've had a packet sitting on the pantry shelf for a rather long time and need a fine excuse to put it to work.

Pat stew meat dry, then salt and pepper it. Heat olive oil in a large, heavy pot over medium-high heat. Brown ⅓ of the stew meat until the outside gets nice and brown, about 2 minutes. (Turn it as it browns.) Remove the meat from the pot with a slotted spoon and put on a plate or in a bowl. Add the rest of the meat, in thirds, to the pot and brown it, too. Remove to the same plate or bowl; set aside.

Add the leeks, onion, and garlic to the pot, stirring to coat in all the brown bits at the bottom. Cook for 2 minutes, then add the carrots and cremini mushrooms and, again, cook for a few minutes. Add tomato paste and anchovies (secret ingredient number I) to the pot. Stir it into the alliums and vegetables and cook for 2 more minutes.

Meanwhile, soak dried porcini mushrooms (secret ingredient number 2) in I cup warm water.

Add wine vinegar (secret ingredient number 3) and tomatoes with juice. Pour in the beef broth, stirring constantly. Add salt, bay leaves, and thyme and bring to a boil. Stir in porcini mushrooms; then add beef back to the pot, cover, and reduce the heat to low. Simmer, covered, for 1½ to 2 hours.

After 1½ to 2 hours, add the diced carrots, turnips, rutabaga, and parsnip to the pot. Stir to combine, put lid back on the pot, and let simmer for another 45 minutes to 1 hour. (Sauce should be thick, but if it seems too thick, splash in a bit of beef broth until it's to your liking.)

When root vegetables are tender, stir in half the minced parsley. Add salt and pepper to taste. Cool to room temperature. Retire to the fridge for a few hours or overnight. (This peaks deliciousness, I promise, though you could dive in now, hot off the stove, and be mighty delighted.)

Once it's chilled, skim off any fat from the surface. Reheat over low heat, letting the stew simmer 45 minutes to 1 hour before serving.

Serve piping hot with steamy mounds of mashed potatoes, letting the juice run amok. Just before serving, stir in half the remaining minced parsley and use the rest as garnish, sprinkled atop the stew. Sacramental, indeed.

Tending the Clutch: The Healing Balms of Motherhood

Avian nursery: "Once a clutch of eggs is hatched, mama birds (and often fathers) have three all-consuming jobs: keeping the young warm, fed, and clean. The tiniest young make it known when one of these needs is pressing, and the trick is for parents to know which. Before nestlings are feathered out, one parent (often but not always the mother) broods them to keep them warm as the other spends time looking for food and delivering it.

"I've seen baby birds frightened or puzzled by situations and watched the parents work their way through it. I've seen swallow parents hover inches from a baby's face as if saying, 'You can do it!' Or when a Great Blue Heron father delivered a pile of fish and one was still alive, wriggling every time one of the babies reached over to grasp it. And each time it wriggled, the babies all lurched up in obvious shock and fear. He gently picked up the fish and dropped it again, as if reassuring the young that, yep, this really is food. After doing this a few times, one of the babies finally downed the fish.

"One afternoon I sat down watching a Pileated Woodpecker father and daughter in a tree. He would tap on the tree in a spot and pull his head back so she would try, and voilà! There was a bug! He did that several times, but then she started getting impatient, wanting to be fed right this moment, and fluttered her wings and made begging calls. So he dug out a few bugs for her, and then went back to the patient teaching."[1]

—*Laura Erickson, Field Notes*

When Baseballs Break a Heart: A Lesson You Wish a Kid Didn't Need to Learn

On Shattered Dreams and the Question of Mending

The night before, we laid out the uniform. The spic-and-span white pants, the socks and shirt and hat the color of a rubber ducky.

The mitt, nearly sacramental, was laid on top. The final offering, it seemed, to the gods of baseball. Or maybe merely to the patron saints, the ones whose job it was, you'd think, to look down on little diamonds dotted all across America, make sure no hearts were broken. Not needlessly anyway.

When it comes to baseball and hearts, the sound of cracking hardly comes from bats alone, biting into leather-bound balls.

That's pretty much the way it went last Sunday, when the team known as the Plumbers took the field. And walked off five innings later thoroughly, well, tanked.

But that's getting ahead of the ball here.

What happened the other day was, like so much of life, teeter-tottered. One team was made up of little squirts, second graders new at baseball and pitching and hitting without a tee, and the other team was, well, old hands. And huge, by the way. Third graders who'd been around the bases plenty of times.

It was the opening game of the season, in the league the little kids look up to, the first one where you get to don the catcher's garb—the caged helmet, the strap between the legs, the padded shield, oh my—and kids, not coaches, get to pitch.

It's the league of little players' dreams. And just the day before, they'd gathered for as old-fashioned a welcoming ceremony as you could imagine, complete with red-white-and-blue bunting on the outfield fence, fifty-cent doughnut holes, dugouts, and a pledge to "make it fun; above all, make it fun."

Well, before the teams took to the grass and sand-strewn mound, even a rookie like me could tell that somehow something was off-kilter. Felt a bit like Goldilocks, one team too little, the other too, too big.

But it wasn't the kids so much as the coaches who quickly emerged as big, bad bears.

There were two, in particular, on the other team. One, a beefy guy who wore his Big Ten jersey beneath his Little League T-shirt. The other: lean, in khaki trousers, not smiling.

Those coaches took on this game as if it were some sort of season-ending series and their lives and lungs depended on a win.

From the get-go they were whooping and bellowing. Telling one player or another to knock it off. Hustle. Hustle. CHASE THE BALL, KID, WHAT ARE YA THINKIN'?!

Right off, they encouraged stealing bases. A kid would hit, the little Plumbers in the far-out field would fumble for the ball, chase it half a mile, and all the while the other team's coaches would be spinning round their arms, like some cockeyed windmill, fanning in another run.

Didn't take long for the little ones to take on a dazed sort of expression.

Inning after inning it went like this: kids from the other team stepped up to the plate, hit, ran, stole, scored. Ran through the lineup nearly every time.

Scored run after run after run. After run. And that was just the first inning.

Then the little guys got a turn. Three up, three down. Boom, boom, boom. Three strikes, yer out. Three outs, yer on the field.

Pretty soon the score was 20–0.

After an inning or three, we lost count. But those coaches never let up.

They were calling out the batters' names, four or five at a time, assuming, I suppose, that they'd bat forever, without a single out.

Wasn't long before the kids on the other coaches' team picked up on this chest-thumping bravado. They'd bellow out the score from time to time, a pathetic count that rose—on one side only, thank you—like mercury on a steamy August day.

Alas, inning after inning, the little Plumbers stayed stuck at the hollowest of numbers.

"It's 35–0," one kid from the other team called out, in case anyone was listening. Yelled it so loud, I'm fairly certain he was making sure kids two towns away would know the score.

The worst part, though, came hours later. At bedtime. Of course, when all the muddy waters of the day come rushing out, and rinsing needs be done.

My little slugger, no surprise, couldn't fall asleep, and soon had called for help.

"I can't sleep," he yelled in apt description.

Seems the whole darn game, inning after inning, was playing in his head: the fly ball he'd missed, the one that let the batter earn a triple; the strikeout the only time he got to bat; the foul tip that got away.

Wasn't long before the tears came too.

"We lost by forty-three," he said, demonstrating second-grade subtraction skills. "That's half of a hundred," he said, demonstrating wide-eyed approximation.

Demonstrating, too, just how badly it hurt to be a little kid with giant baseball dreams who'd had them thoroughly, undeniably trampled. Rubbed in like grass stains on his once-bleached knees.

Just the night before, this would-be catcher-slash-center-fielder had had trouble falling asleep, what with all the home-run pictures in his head. Heard the crowd roaring, he did. Imagined the coach handing him the little plunger that, each game, goes to the Plumbers' player of the game.

And now, one game later, he'd seen the way it sometimes is: coaches taking on the task as if a win, at any cost, is all that matters. Paying no mind to pint-sized kids and their first outing on the field. Waving in runners twice the size of the little ones fumbling under bushes, trying to throw the ball anywhere in the vicinity of a base.

It hurt, the poor kid said.

He was mad and sad and thoroughly confused: baseball was a game he loved. A game he watched at night, lying beside his papa. A game he read about every morning, slurping statistics along with Frosted Flakes.

And now, because of baseball, he felt, he said, like someone put their baseball cleat right where his heart goes thump, and then, with all their weight, they'd clomped on it.

It hurt, he said again. In case I'd missed the obvious.

And then, at last, he drifted off toward sleep.

His mitt, that night, was nowhere near his bed. He'd dumped it as soon as he came in the door. His yellow hat, though, hung on the post of his bed.

He wasn't giving up.

Just poring over pages in the playbook, trying to figure out the game.

And so is his mama.

Trying to figure out just how to salve the sting of hardball played too soon. And what's the wisest stance when life throws fouls? Or the lessons hurled knock you back a pace or two?

Sure thing, I'll need to find a way to dust him off or, better yet, point him toward some saving grace, some truth, to steady him, to remind him, after all, it's not the final score that shows you who the winner is.

For now, though, all I know is this: when I walked in that night, to kiss him one last time, his cheek was soggy still. He'd cried himself to sleep.

The Sum of Infinites

On the Litany of Loving, No Matter How Infinitesimal the Measures

The last time I'd seen him—when I tucked him into bed, blew a kiss, and closed the door—he was fine. Just really tired, he said, worn out by soccer. And rumblingly hungry.

But next morning, as I walked out of the downtown parking garage, fumbled for the ringing rectangle in my backpack, tried to find a place to plop the coffee mug so I could walk and talk and think out loud, I heard the words, "Mr. T. is not feeling so good. He's pretty hot, actually. And his throat, he says, is killing him."

A series of arrangements was duly rearranged, numbers dialed, summons pleaded, before I even spied my desk.

Given precise instruction, exact latitude and longitude of where he'd find the white and orange and azure box on the bathroom shelf, his papa dispensed the first round of fever-queller, tucked him back into bed, then kept a finger in the dike until dear Grammy could ride to the rescue.

Miles away, I was but a distant player, so my part had me checking in every chance I got. Or so we'd scripted. Until I got the call mid afternoon, and a squeaky little voice informed me, "I'm dizzy." Then asked, "When can Mama come home?"

NOW! was pretty much the word that popped into my head, so I cleared my desk and drove. And once through the blue front door, I dropped my keys and lunged and kissed him on the head.

Oh, the look in those empty eyes told me all I needed in the medical data department. Those of us who've trodden this ground need no compass, no thermometer; we know by heart these dark and murky woods, know by gut just how deep we're in and how the road out will be a slow and bumpy one.

And thus began, again, the work of one mama tending to her achy, fevered little person.

By rapid—and rough—calculation, I'd guess this might have been the ninetieth such round, each one with its own odd particulars, since I'd first put on the mama robes, since boy number one was born, so many, many fevers ago.

As I spent the long night dispensing care in the ways my boys have grown to know, to count on, I began to contemplate how love, especially motherlove, is the sum of infinites.

Minute, and barely perceptible, although wholly definable and defining, they are the accumulated brushstrokes and palm presses and finger squeezes that imprint, somehow, on the souls of those whose care—whose fevered limbs, swollen glands, fractured bones, woopsy tummies—we cradle.

Until the fever lifts, the gland goes down, the tummy stops its gurgling, we dole out and dispense our ministrations without surrender to our own bodies' begging for unbroken sleep, or just a chair, or even a bowl of oatmeal that hasn't gone cold.

It is the umpteen blankets and pillows you've piled on the floor in that certain way you've come to call "The Nest."

It is the 181 washcloths hauled off the shelf, doused under cool water, wrung out, folded, and laid on fevered brow.

It is the ninety-nine rubber bands stretched around just as many glasses, each one marking it a badge of courage for the sick one, and off-limits besides—lest you hastily find yourself tending a whole flock of fevered lambs.

It's the way, without a moment's pause, and no thought given to germs or contagion, you've climbed three thousand times right into bed beside the hot one, so you are there should there be a whimper in the night, should you need to totter down the stairs one time or ten to fill a glass with ice, with honey, with 7UP, with gooey purple fever-buster. Or just because the ailing one left a certain pillow on the couch—and cannot sleep without it.

It is the who-knows-how-many baths you've drawn at three in the morning, because the fever won't go down and the little arms and legs you once marveled at, now barely ever eyeballed beneath the sweatshirts and the soccer shin guards, are shaking like a leaf that barely clings to the branch amid October's bluster.

Next morn, as you hear the doctor speak the words, "Go straight to the ER"—thank God you can count (three) the times you've heard that command—you realize that your well will never run dry, that you would pierce the microbes with sharp spear, given half a chance. That you would climb on the gurney, slide your own wobbly self through that CT scan, stick out your own arm to take the IV needles, you would wrestle to the mud whatever pokes and prods come your little one's way, as you wipe away the tears and kiss the red-hot cheeks and hold your breath and wait for all-clear whistles from the ER nurse, the one you now worship because she was so gentle in her poking of your little soldier's brave, brave arm.

You realize, as you add up the hours of the week and lose count of ice cubes and teaspoons of germ-killer, that these hidden-away devotions, the ones played out over sickbeds or hunched beside toilet bowls, are no less heroic than the conquests of champions, the ones that steal headlines.

And that in the end, when all these flus and streps and bacterial pneumonias are past, we will have loved our way to triumph, in a race without a ribbon, a contest with no starting gun, an Olympiad we enter with our heart.

It is through the sum of infinitely loving, and infinite signature touches, that the little ones whose flesh and blood and coos and cries we were handed not so long ago will grow up wholly defining how it is to be ministered to, to be loved, to be—yes—mothered, no matter who the motherer.

And—as you've maybe glimpsed once or twice already, when you're the one who's down and your little ones begin to mimic all your ways—they in turn will love as you have loved, will fold the same cool cloths, draw the baths, pour the ginger ale, stir the chicken noodle soup.

And thus our unmeasurable infinite acts will go forth into infinity.

A mighty sum—born, simply, out of love.

Sometimes We Forget the Power of a Hug

On Being Embraced

It was last Friday night, I am nearly certain, when my little one, who sometimes is a prophet, climbed into our bed. He wanted snuggles, he said.

And then, as he was wrapped from both sides by arms that have harbored him since that long-ago hot August night when his eight whopping pounds first slipped upon us, he spoke the words that have blanketed me all week:

"I like when you hug me. I feel like the whole world is around me, and I feel like nothing could ever hurt me."

I know that's what he said, because as he spoke in that pure-hearted voice of a boy who doesn't censor a syllable, the words—a mere two dozen swiftly chosen, unfiltered words—pried open my heart, whirled to that place where they will forever live, and I let out a sigh.

It's not every night you find yourself wrapped around poetry.

"I like when you hug me. I feel like the whole world is around me, and I feel like nothing could ever hurt me."

I am certain those are the words he spoke because I wasn't about to leave anything to chance, there in the dark. Or to the soft spots in my memory.

I asked for the phone (yes, in the dark). I dialed my number at work. And I recited the words into the phone, knowing I'd etched them into the digital memory that is my work voicemail.

That sweet little boy didn't know—nor did any of us—how powerful those words would forever ring, especially as they came just twelve hours before a madman in Tucson, Arizona, lifted a gun called a Glock (a name that sends shivers down my spine, the sound of cold-blooded crime locked in its clipped, hard-edged consonants), and sprayed bullets into a crowd, into the heart—yes, the heart—of a nine-year-old child.

"I like when you hug me. I feel like the whole world is around me, and I feel like nothing could hurt me."

So we hold our breath and pray.

So we wish.

So we fool ourselves every time we wrap our arms around the ones we love.

As if it's a shield that cannot be shattered. As if impenetrable walls are forever wrapped around the ones we love, the vulnerable ones, the ones who do not—do not—have rhyme or reason to be taken away.

Lord, have mercy.

My little boy's words, now a refrain I tumble round my brain, like some succulent fruit whose juice I cannot get enough of, his words are what we pray for.

His words are what we need to remember.

Isn't that the prayer at the heart of all our comings and goings?

"I like when you hug me. I feel like the whole world is around me, and I feel like nothing could hurt me."

We are, sadly, old enough and battered enough to understand the limits of those words, a child's words, to run our fingers along the sharp edge where our prayers fall off and pure chance reigns.

But the words are worth remembering: it's our place in the world, our place by the gift of being grown-ups, to wrap our arms around our children, around all those we love, the ones whose breath we depend on, the ones whose stirrings matter.

It is all our children ask of us, in the end, to be their shields from the darkness, to chase away the ghosts and goblins, the creaks in the hall in the thick of the night, the ones that scare them to no end.

Motherprayer

They lean their little bodies into us, into our soft chests. They ask for so little: *Wrap me, make me feel safe, shoosh away the monsters.*

And while there might always be madmen, and madwomen, who steal the light, who shatter the morning's hope, our jobs do not cease.

Our arms are forever needed, and the hearts that beat in the middle:

"I like when you hug me. I feel like the whole world is around me, and I feel like nothing could hurt me."

It just might be our most important job: hug the ones you love today. Pray with all your might that you can keep them safe—from harm, from hurt, from monsters.

Even when they don't put words to it; the little prophet reminded me the other night in the shadow of the darkness.

Humpty Dumpty Powder and Other Potions of Motherhood

On Putting Our Children Together Again

Humpty Dumpty had a great fall. All the king's horses and all the king's men couldn't put Humpty together again.

Indeed, and thank goodness, not all the falls that befall our little ones are great ones.

Sometimes, they're bumps.

Sometimes brought on by being brave in the woods. Sometimes by being brave in the woods for two long weeks you thought might never end. Sometimes they're stirred by spending the night in a tent on the side of a sand dune, on a night when the thunder and lightning would not cease, when hail pummeled the tent flaps, when the counselors at 3 a.m. shooshed you onto the bus for safekeeping while they struggled to stake down the flipped-over tents, and all you could manage was to pray for dawn's first light and a cure for the ache in your belly.

And so, when you get to the end of that shell-shaking spell in the woods, when your mama pulls up to the dried meadow at the edge of camp and you leap out of your flip-flops to throw yourself into her arms, you need your mama to reach deep into her bag of mama tricks and pull out the Humpty Dumpty powder.

You need your mama to put you together again.

That's what mamas do best. That's job number one in the Old Mama Bible.

Oh, sure we birth those babes back at the launch. But from then on, it's our supreme holy calling to be there for bee stings and dog bites and nights without end in the woods.

And it is indeed how I am spending these hours, ever since I picked up my brave little camper there in the woods.

Didn't take long, not more than a minute, to see that this hadn't quite been a picnic, no mere frolic on the shores of Torch Lake. And it wasn't simply the stench coming from his toes, there in the back of the homeward-bound rescue mobile.

There were clues, the sort a mama can read without prompt, that the boy sound asleep for most of the car ride, straight through Michigan and half of Indiana, had utterly and completely tapped out his stay-strong tank.

Heck, he'd survived on PB&J for the better part of thirteen lunches and thirteen dinners. Even the night of the all-camp banquet, when ribs and baked Alaska highlight the menu, the boy I love filled up on "four ears of corn and candy." His words, exactly.

No wonder he came home sun-browned and skinny.

So, besides the bottle of bleach and the buckets for multiple presoaks (half the loam of the woods came home stuck in our sweet camper's socks), we have pulled out all stops here on the home-team recovery squad.

We've showered him with kisses and filled the bathtub with bubbles. We've cooked up cherry-filled pancakes, drizzled cherry syrup over slabs of turkey bacon, concocted "Torch Lake sunrises," an orange-juice-and-cherry-concentrate breakfast mocktail.

We've squeezed triple-antibiotic ointment into oozing blisters on the sides of both feet. We've fluffed a pillow, unfurled a blanket and rubbed itty-bitty circles there where the headache pounded.

But the best cure of all was the big brother who'd once roamed the same woods, downed the same baked Alaska. He knew the camp songs, the lore, the legend. He got the kid laughing again.

Come dinnertime, we let the little guy order up a feast of favorites:

made-from-scratch mac and cheese, ditto the applesauce, corn on the cob (minus the candy, his mama insisted), chased with cherry pie à la mode.

In no time, we suspect, our little camper ought to be back to his usual mostly unflappable self.

But one of the breathtaking truths of motherhood is that you've got a rare, front-row seat on the naked work of growing up and learning to be brave.

I'll never forget that kid standing at the window, just two weeks ago, the night before we left him at camp. He was staring up to the starlit dome, and, even there in the dark, you could read the prayers spill off his lips, and the way he wrapped it all up with a sign of the cross and a tip of his palm to the heavens, just as the ballplayers do. He was beside himself with worry, he told us. Could not imagine going two weeks without seeing a glimpse of us.

But he made it. He did it.

And that's what I keep whispering in his ear.

"You did it, sweetheart. You did the very thing you thought you couldn't."

And if, for the next couple of days, we need to stoke you with buckets of cherries and lavish you with kisses, we'll get you steady on your feet. Because we've seen you, backlit by the night sky, in your hour of near-despair, and we've felt our own lungs swell at the depth of your courage: you took to the woods, little one, and you found your way home, shaken but not cracked.

Tables Turned

On the Breathtaking Wonder of Discovering That Hearts Have Been Listening, and Lessons Learned

Since Tuesday, I've had a fever. I've been achy all over, and moving slow as slow can be yet still qualify as movement.

I've even taken to my mattress a couple of afternoons, which—around here—is unheard of. But the most amazing thing unfolded one of those afternoons, the first one when I was stretched out and aching and hotter than hot. A young lad came to my bedside and insisted he was the fever fixer. He had a plan, he said, and he set out to execute.

From down the stairs and around the bend, I heard the clunk of ice cubes being procured. I heard the linen closet squeaking open. I heard the old metal tray being pulled from where we store those sorts of things. And then I heard the hobbling sound of my sweet boy—the one with one leg in a brace and one arm in a cast, thanks to a terrible tumble over his handlebars, week before last—I heard him climbing the stairs.

He appeared at my bedside on a hot July afternoon bearing a tray that held a dripping wet washcloth, a cup of ice chips, and an apple perched pertly in a white soufflé cup. Before I could say a word, he slipped his castless hand into the puppet of a washcloth, one of those terry-towel hand puppets meant to make bath time for little ones a theater of suds.

This particular washcloth, the one that was always his favorite, happens to be a hippo. So my bedside attendant stretched wide the hippo's mouth, grabbed two cubes of ice, and proceeded to anoint my forehead in this icy, dripping bath. Next, he reached for my wrists, and up and down my arms and legs. "You'll be OK," were the only words he whispered the whole long while. Over and over, he repeated, "You'll be OK," as if the words alone were incantations, as if a prayer aloud.

A few minutes into this anointing of the sick, I finally mustered the breath to ask: "Who taught you this?"

His answer: "You."

I felt a tear roll down my cheek. It's true, yes, that a wet washcloth applied to fevered brow has long been wielded here for curative effect. And ice chips in a cup, often dripped with honey, has long been an apothecary staple in this old house. But never in my life have I been as gentle, as determined, as tender as that boy was to me. The tenderness he learned from his papa. Of that I'm certain. I, too, am learning tenderness—all these years later—from my sweet boy's papa. It's a lesson without end.

While the icy rinse didn't make the fever go away, it decidedly worked wonders. For days now, my sweet boy has attended me with his hippo and his ice cubes. I asked him amid one of the icy rubdowns if he'd ever thought of being a doctor or a nurse, because he certainly had the healer's touch. Nope, said he, explaining, "I don't like blood, and I'm not good at science."

The marvel here is that we often think the long nights we've spent on bathroom floors with a retching or fevered child, the midnight hours when we're the ones knocking ice cubes from the freezer, we think of those, sometimes, as invisible hours, times that draw no notice. What we might not realize is that in that transactional moment, when ice practically sizzles on a fevered brow, when a kid so sick he can barely open his droopy lids lets us slip an ice chip to his tongue, what we're doing is so much more than knocking back a fever. We are quietly, and without folderol, teaching something sacred to the essence of being human. Maybe fevers and flus were invented for the simple purpose of one someone being invited to try to heal another.

The marvel here—the reminder that came in dripping ice cubes this week—is that a life-and-death curriculum is unfurling here in the quiet of our humdrum little lives. Our whole life long we are teaching and learning that most magnificent of golden rules: love as you would be loved.

Not a minute is wasted. Not a lesson lost. Little folk and big folk alike are paying attention, our hearts attuned to those gifts, those moments, that lift us, inch by inch, to a higher plane. We love, and so we are loved in kind.

I remembered this week that I am ever teaching, and lessons are ever being learned, even when I don't think a single soul notices, nor pays attention. So I'd best try to live as tenderly, as full of heart, as my sweet child is teaching me to be.

That kid and his ice cubes, they more than did their job. In fact, they melted me. And my fever, too.

From the Cookery Files...

When the bee stings, or the homesick blues need quelling, this oozy spoonful of deliciousness belongs in a mama's tin of kitchen cure-alls. It's the ubiquitous remedy at our house for any ailment in the book. (And one or two make-believe ones, besides.)

When All Else Fails...Turn to Page 200

Two decades ago, when I was plotting my firstborn's second birthday fete, I flipped open the pages of my monthly infusion of delicious, *Gourmet* magazine, and landed on page 200. Since then, that page has pretty much been my no-fail, last-ditch, best-hope-of-filling-a-hole-in-a-heart-by-way-of-the-belly cookery map. After twenty years, the magazine's binding is coming unglued, the page now crusted with splatters of roux. No matter; by now, I know my way. Nearly by heart. It's a page that plies its magic any day, really, in any season, but especially so on a crisp autumnal day, when the amber sunlight pours in. And so it was on a recent day when the boy who'd loped to the car at the schoolhouse curb was a boy with a leaden heart. He had so much homework, was so worried about homework, that he'd decided to skip the end-of-the-season soccer gorge on pasta and pizza. Instead of hanging with friends, he'd decided he should come straight home after practice.

So I reached for my holy salvation: the plainly named "Baked Macaroni and Cheese," à la page 200. It's a cheesy-buttery bath stirred round and through tubes of wide-mouthed pasta, each tube filling with ooze as much as being wrapped in it. It vies, in our house, with bread pudding as the neck-and-neck numbers one and two comforts on a spoon.

Over the years, the making of it—for me, anyway—is as soothing as it must be for my boys to polish it off in one sitting. Assembling its components—the butter, cheddar, flour, milk, salt, paprika, bread crumbs, and Parmesan shavings to finish it off—I slip into priestess mode. My old black cookstove—an industrial-grade contraption that somehow slipped into this old house in the 1970s, never to be removed—is my altar.

I begin my incantations and prestidigitations right there, where the flame is cranked, and the concoctions in my pots begin to bubble, not unlike vats of heavenly potions. With the oven cranked to 375, the kitchen begins to warm. Everything about this kitchen ritual is warming. Soon, my old sweater is off, and as I stir I imagine my sweet boy coming home to find the big white ceramic soufflé dish perched atop the stove.

Is there a more certain way to say I love you than to have cooked all afternoon? To have reached for the cookery shelf and pulled out the one thing a kid asks for on those nights when his sleepy head hits the pillow but the worries won't be extinguished?

Provenance: Gourmet *magazine, May 1995*

Yield: Serves 8 children

3 tablespoons unsalted butter
3½ tablespoons all-purpose flour
½ teaspoon paprika
3 cups milk
1 teaspoon salt
¾ pound pasta, tubes or wagon wheels or whatever shape
    suits your fancy (a tube—penne or rigatoni, among
    the many—fills with the cheesy sauce and makes a fine,
    pillowy bite)
10 ounces sharp cheddar cheese, shredded coarse (about 2¾
    cups)

I cup fresh bread crumbs, coarse
¼ cup (or more) Parmesan shavings

Preheat oven to 375 degrees Fahrenheit, and butter a 2-quart shallow baking dish (the broader the crust, the better).

In a 6-quart pot, bring 5 quarts salted water to a boil for cooking pasta.

In a heavy saucepan, melt butter over moderately low heat and stir in flour and paprika. Cook roux, whisking, 3 minutes; then whisk in milk and salt. Bring sauce to a boil, whisking, and simmer, whisking occasionally, 3 minutes. Remove pan from heat.

Stir pasta into pot of boiling water and boil, stirring occasionally, until *al dente*. Drain pasta in a colander, and in a large bowl stir together pasta, sauce, and 2 cups cheddar cheese. Transfer mixture to prepared dish. *Macaroni and cheese may be prepared up to this point 1 day ahead and chilled, covered tightly (an indispensable trick when confronting a serious to-do list for a day of birthday jollity).*

In a small bowl, toss remaining ¾ cup cheddar with bread crumbs and sprinkle over pasta mixture, topping it all with a downpour of Parmesan shavings (a heavy hand with the cheese is never a bad thing, certainly not at my house where my boys insist I do so, preferring their cheese to supersede bread crumbs).

Bake macaroni and cheese in middle of oven for 25 to 30 minutes, or until golden and bubbling. Let stand 10 minutes before serving. At last: dig in.

Nestling: At the Edge of the Nest

nestling: *(n.)* Late fourteenth century: a "bird too young to leave the nest"; etymological roots in Proto-Indo-European, *nizdo*, probably from *ni* (down) + *sed* (to sit).[1]

A young, recently hatched bird that has not yet grown any flight feathers and is unable to fly. They may lack feathers entirely or could be covered with a light down, depending on the species. Nestling birds are entirely dependent on their parents for food and protection, though the length of that dependency varies for each bird species from just a few days to several weeks.[2]

Waiting

On Learning to Sink into the Downy Comfort of Midnight's Vigil

I kept an eye on that full moon of a clock, the one that peers down from over the door of the kitchen. The minute hand seemed to be moving like mud through molasses. Or maybe it was up there taking a bit of a snooze.

After all, it was minutes away from midnight—the deepest dark hour, nadir of the night.

And the child I'd last seen a few hours ago, when I dropped him off at the curb in the snow and the glow of a street lamp, well, he was out coursing the roads, a friend at the wheel, the roads getting icy, and I was there in the kitchen thrumming my fingers, pretending to read, but really I wasn't paying one bit of attention. Not to the book sprawled before me, anyway.

My attention, instead, was rather devoted to the hands of the clock and the knob on the door whose click I was straining to hear, if only I willed it intensely enough.

Someone's home, it would say. The someone you wanted to see is safe now, is here. Is back from the place where you have utterly no control. Where cars can cross lines and odd things can happen. Where outcomes are wholly, eternally, always, left to fat chance.

Not home. Not here in the scope of your eyes and your ears where you can be a little more certain—if not guaranteed, not even at all—that all will be well.

Motherprayer

And so in the abyss that plunges between those two cliffs—uncertainty and certainty—I engaged in the ancient and timeless art of waiting.

To wait, sometimes, is to be pregnant with hope. Sometimes, to wait is to dread. But that's not the case, not really, when it's a child you birthed, fourteen short years ago, who is out in the world, and it's dark and it's late and you would like once again to hear the clomp of his feet sloshing snow on the rug in the hall.

To this particular species of waiting, you realize quickly, you are quite new, quite unaccustomed. You only just now are getting a taste of the trials that come with the letting out of the spool that, until now, until high school, you kept rather close to the palm of your hand.

The art of waiting for someone you love, someone to please come home, is an art that has lost some of its power here in the day of the cellular tether. Worried? Give a call. Can't find? Cell can.

Back through the history of time, though, there has been waiting and waiting. Penelope waited for Odysseus. Civil War mothers waited for soldier sons. And now I, a mother whose son had just lost his cell phone, waited for mine.

Odd thing, the book that was waiting with me, the book I was allegedly reading, the book whose words my eyes glanced at but didn't take in, not so much anyway, was a book with a passage on waiting.

As the clock ticked ever so slowly, I passed again over the letters spilled there on the page.

This time I read:

> Waiting, because it will always be with us, can be made a work of art, and the season of Advent invites us to underscore and understand with a new patience that very feminine state of being, waiting.
>
> Our masculine world wants to blast away waiting from our lives....We equate waiting with wasting. So we build Concorde airplanes, drink instant coffee, roll out green plastic and call it turf, and reach for the phone before we reach for the pen. The more life asks us to wait, the more we anxiously hurry.[3]

The author of these words is Gertrud Mueller Nelson, whose 1986 book, *To Dance with God*, is a treatise on ritual and one of those rare books that offers more, plentiful more, with each reading.

She encourages us to practice the art of waiting, the art of delayed gratification. Our children, most of all, need to practice and practice, she urges. And this time before Christmas, this time when the world is rushing so madly, she suggests in a deep counter-cultural challenge, is the peak time to settle in and make the most of the incubation that begs our attention.

"Brewing, baking, simmering, fermenting, ripening, germinating, gestating are the feminine processes of becoming and they are the symbolic states of being which belong in a life of value, necessary to transformation," Nelson writes.

And I listen.

Is not the slowing of time, and the quickening of attention, the whole point of our practice here? Are we not, day after day, looking to slow the E-Z, the instant, the world without pause?

Are we not working to learn to cup in our hands the holiest waters of life as they're poured? Might we not look to the Monarch butterfly, who alights on the milkweed amid his long flight, who settles and sips, who quells for a moment his orange-speckled flittering? Aren't we, too, trying to stop, take a drink, quench the unquenchable thirst?

What, then, to do with the minutes near midnight, when the child you love, the child just starting to be off on his own, finding his way in the dark, isn't yet home?

I suppose I could fritter away the slow-moving minutes. Picture the car on the side of the road. The children jolting. The call that couldn't be dialed.

Or, I could sink down to a deeper place in my heart. I could rumble around, think of the ways that he keeps me in stitches. Think of the light in his eyes. Picture the mop of his curls. Remember the rhythm with which he plucked on his big double bass, there at the edge of the stage just hours ago, when the light happened to shine and catch the tops of his curls.

I could take hold of the minutes of waiting and savor the blessing of beholding the boy I love. I could practice the art of filling with hope. Being pregnant to life's possibilities, the ones that take time, take no shortcut.

I could ripen to love.

And when the click of the door comes, and the slosh of the very big shoes, I could sigh.

The long wait is over. Amen.

One Thing—Be Safe

On What Matters Most, Ever and Always

*A*nd so, like that, hair still wet from the shower, white T-shirt tight enough to catch each plane and shadow of the rower's top-half topography, the babe I once rocked in my arms, the boy who never much took to tricycles, the now-man with newly minted license in his tight-squeeze pocket, he did something I'd never seen before: he swiped the keys to the old blue wagon off the ring where they've dangled since the day we moved into this old house, and he ran for the door, for the driver's seat, for the road and whatever lay beyond.

Midstride and without ceremony, he glanced back to check the clock, nervously (only because he was late, not because he had an ounce of apprehension about the road ahead), as I tried to slow the exit, calling out, "Wait, where exactly are you going? And when will you be home?"

As he tossed back words, perfectly sensible replies, and made one final lope through the door and down the steps, disappearing behind the crab apple that nearly blocks the path, I called out: "Be safe."

And the words hung there.

Each crisp syllable so wholly capturing what I wished and prayed for with all my being.

Be safe.

What more is there?

What deeper prayer does a mother's heart hold?

Above all, be safe.

Come home whole. Come home without a gash. Never mind the fender or the taillights. Just be safe, my sweet, beloved child.

And so for the next few hours, I went about my business. Few noticed, I'm certain, that I was turning blue around the mouth. I held my breath. Only half expanding lungs, I do believe, as I watched the hour hand glide toward ten.

Until at last I heard the rumble, saw the headlights illuminating garbage cans as they pointed down the alley and came round the final bend into where we sometimes park the car, two bright eyeballs blinking, *We're home*, as they clicked off, and the six-foot-three first-time-*ever*-alone driver slid from the old wagon as if he'd been out unencumbered a million times before and this was nothing, nothing really to have interrupted anyone's lung-work for the eve.

I find myself employing those two words—*be safe*—often in these past few weeks.

Both my boys, it seems, are pushing out the boundaries, laying new tracks, expanding their orbits beyond me. Out of reach. Into that terrain where we hold on only through the silky thread of prayer, the whispered murmurings of petition to the great protectors all around, or up on clouds, wherever is the place from which they keep their watch.

The little one now bounds up the stairs to his piggy bank, grabs a crumpled dollar bill, and tells me he is walking to the not-so-far-away ma-and-pa grocery where all the kids buy chips and candy. Or to the comic book store. Or, just the other day, over train tracks, across the big street, the one with five lanes of traffic, to the store where baseballs called to his friend, and my little one didn't think to say, "Um, no, I can't come with you without checking first at home."

And as he sweetly told the story—confessed, really—I could only gulp and think of *safe* again, that word that captures unbroken wholeness, the white light of safety shield that we hope and pray and beg surrounds our children, no matter what they throw against it: diving boards or busy streets or big rigs with drivers half-dozing at the wheel.

Not one to rely on hope alone, and having grown up with rosary beads dangling from my bedpost, at the bottom of my white straw pocketbook (the one with starched-cotton cornflowers and poppies on the lid, the one I carried each Sunday into church), and, yes, amid the pens and pencils and assorted detritus in the pit of my high school backpack besides, I wasted little time before enlisting Saint Christopher to my back-up squad.

I ordered up a medallion, a dangly disc, of dear saintly Chris, the one who carried baby Jesus (I do believe) on his shoulders across a raging river, and who, along with Saint Babs, my namesake, got unceremoniously dumped from the heavenly chorus back in the revolutionary 1960s when the Catholic Church decided their miracles weren't quite of saintly stature, so they were stripped of rank, left to be mere lieutenants of goodness in the hierarchy's eyes. Which, of course, is all it took for me to promptly and fiercely promote them ever higher, in my book now patron saints of all of us who have ever suffered the indignities of being shoved to the back of the pack.

Yo, Chris, for you we have an assignment.

And thus, in a white envelope left waiting on my keyboard (thanks be to my own personal patron saint of procuring—my holy blessed mama, who knows where to find these things), there is now the half-inch metal oval of midstream Chris that will forever dangle from my brand-new driver's key ring.

Be safe, it will whisper, will send off vapors, will infuse the air my first-born breathes when he is far, far beyond my clutch.

Be safe, the holy mantra of the mamas, as we stand back and let our babies reach and stretch and take to the highways. Saint Chris, right there in that front pocket, where we could never squeeze in.

Sometimes...

On the Hours When You Have No Answers

Sometimes, when you're a mama, you wish you could fix it all with an apple cut into crescent moons, an oozy grilled cheese, and a wee mug filled with chocolate-stirred milk, those bits of kitchen balm that once upon a time fixed a skinned knee, a broken toy, or a bad day at kindergarten.

Sometimes, when you're a mama, it's nowhere so easy.

Sometimes, say the night your firstborn promised the college essays would be done—signed, sealed, delivered—when you find yourself checking the status, oh, every half hour. And it's not too long until you realize this night could unravel right before your eyes.

And soon enough, you feel the weight of the world that bears down on the shoulders of the babe you birthed to this world.

And as you sit there listening, sopping up heartache—his and, quickly, your own—you see in your mind's eye the whole picture show of his life.

Frame after frame spilling by.

And stunningly, awesomely, you grasp the enormity of the fact that you've been there for a front-row seat all the way along. And you cannot think of one other someone you have known so through-and-through wholly—every night fever and rash, every scuffle and pitfall. The girl who said no to the dance. And the one who this summer said yes.

And, by now slid down against the chair where he is curled, your shoulder against the sides of his thick rower's legs, you think back to the hours and months before he was born.

Motherprayer

You remember when your belly got to the brink of a room, any room, before the rest of you did. And how you loved that belly. How you tried on the clothes that would show it off, well before you needed to wear them. Because, after waiting a lifetime, you could wait not one minute longer.

You wanted this more than anything ever—before or since.

And you remember, back then, how you promised yourself, promised the unborn babe, promised the universe, and God too, that you would love that sweet not-yet-met someone so wholly and so completely, surround that sweet someone in such an un-pierce-able bubble of love, that babe would never be knocked back by the high waves of doubt and despair that, too often, threatened to topple over you—and did, more than just once.

And you really thought, back then, that committing to love was all it would take.

So you set out to make it come true.

Why, you'd practically worn that babe on your chest, barely put him down (or so your mother chided you), slept curled right beside him. You'd hardly gone out (not on the town, certainly), rarely brought in a sitter. You'd worked from home, given up the downtown office—just to be minutes away, always.

You had done everything under the sun, for years and years and years, to keep that child from knowing the heartache that you could not bear to imagine.

The heartache that now seeped into the room, filling it like a hose with a spigot, as you sit there on a cold autumn night, watching him struggle to type, staring into a screen that resists being filled with his thoughts, with his words, with his sketchpad for college.

You hear a depth of heartache that rips your own right out from your chest. And so, when the talking is done, you cannot walk back to your bed. You cannot leave his room, you realize.

You can't type the words, can't pull the thoughts from the utterly drained mind that is his—he's been at it for days now.

But you can't sleep down the hall. So you do what mamas do, some-times. You stay where you feel the pull.

You curl up on the floor. Lay your head on the emptied-out backpack, make like it's the pillow.

And you close your eyes while the typing starts up again, the pads of his fingers tapping their way toward college.

And you feel the tears roll down your cheeks from under your closed eyelids. You taste the salt of the runaway one that rolls over your lips. You wipe it away before it's noticed.

Once upon a time you thought you could love your child free from all this. Safe from all of this.

And at every turn along the way, you did what you thought would stoke him with strength, with joy, with lightness of heart.

But then on a dark night at the end of October, when all the colleges begged their assignments, you realized that, sometimes, in the end, all you can do is lie there and pray.

And wait for the dawn, finally, to come.

Pushing Buttons

On Watching Life's Frames Unspool

*L*ike that, the other eve, index finger reached and pressed the touchpad: college, applied for.

After all the years and months and weeks. After all the dinner conversations about this class or that. This grade or that. This trip to here or there. After endless hours typing essays. After calculating GPAs, weighted and unweighted, it was a click barely audible.

So much transpired in that fraction of a second, the pushing down, the weight of finger pad against the brushed silver touchpad of the laptop.

If not for my eyes that misted up on cue, if not for the galumph that might have walloped in my firstborn's heart, you'd not have known how much had just occurred.

How much of one boy's life had been condensed into five short essays, a page or two of transcripts, a data sheet of name, address, and biographic stripped-down who-when-where.

And so it is in life: we lift a foot and put it down in a whole new chapter, one that measures mere inches away but in fact is miles and miles from where we started, or where we might have gone.

We say, "I do," and suddenly we are a someone we have never been.

The doctor yells, "Push," and next thing we know we are head over heels in love—not with fuzzy outlines of a dream, but deep, dark eyes that pore over us as if they've always known us, known us since the dawn of time. How can that be, so new and old at once?

We grab a door handle and walk into a workplace that will be our daily exercise for years and years to come.

We drive past a house, slow to an idle, open a car door, meander up the walk, and there we are inside the walls and windows that will be the ones we call home until the day we die.

Thresholds aren't such noisy things, don't come with clanging cymbals or chiming bells.

But in your heart, oh yes, you know you've made the crossing.

So it was the other eve.

I could not shake it the whole next day after my firstborn clicked the college button. Nor that night, when my dreams came boldly and jarringly. I kept reading college essays, all through the discombobulating dreams. I recall papers being pulled from my hands. I'd not finished reading but the page was yanked away.

Maybe, come to think of it, that's how a mother feels when she is trying to wrap her head around the notion that her firstborn will soon be going away, for semesters at a time: *Wait, I'm not done yet. There is more to write, more to read, more to teach and learn. More to love.*

I've not yet gotten to the point where I worry of all the things I've not yet added to his list of I-can-do-its: hospital corner on the bed sheets; ironing a shirt collar without singeing your fingers; getting out of bed without a bucket of water being poured over your sleepy face.

No, I spent the whole day-after simply trying to wrap my head—and the deep-inside part of my soul—round the fact that we now have a kid who has actually applied to college. Done. Did it.

Where'd the years go?

Weren't we just racing out the door, little backpack on his three-year-old shoulders, late to preschool (mere preamble for a life of racing out the door, on the brink of late more often than I care to count)?

What about that little-boy sing-song voice that I still have saved on my phone machine at work, the one from back when he was two and called my office phone to practice asking what time I might be home (even though I only worked one flight of stairs away)?

And further back still, where went the endless days when I cringed at five o'clock for I knew the crying would begin any minute, the unsettled bellyaching that could be soothed only by running water from the bath and rocking in my arms until those biceps yelped to drop the load?

I held on. Through all of it, I managed to hold on.

And now it's ancient history.

But not so long ago that I can't remember.

There is, this year, so much rewinding of the skeins of life, flowing back and forth in time. Trying to grasp, retrace the years. Like a crooked finger put to a map, tracing the route along blue highways, red interstates, how'd we get from here to there?

Some of us like road maps.

Some of us trace and retrace, sift through grains of hours, minutes, months.

Some of us mark time in loops, forward and rewind.

We come to deeper understandings of where we are in time, by circling all around our lives and the lives of the ones we love, to measure and mark just how we got here.

It is as if in sifting, resifting, I am holding up each blessed frame of the time we have had so far. I am holding it up to the light. I am marveling. I am soaking one last drop.

I am savoring.

I am stunned.

The buttons have been pushed now. One more to go before the waiting starts in full pursuit.

And as the year unspools, I will keep close watch, forward and reverse, circling round and looking top to bottom.

I will live and relive the chapters we have had, so when he leaves, I'll know I have savored every drop.

Freeze Frame

On Savoring This Holy Script Called Life

I am holding on to moments, freezing frames, as if compiling a loop of Kodacolor film I will hold, rub my thumbs along, raise up to the light, memorize, when he is gone.

I am stopping at the edge of his room, soaking in the tableau—the jumbled socks, the soggy towel—knowing that in half a year, there will be no messy room.

I am driving to his school, climbing stairs, entering the gallery where his art hangs on the wall. I am standing, neck tilted back, looking up, eyes wide, soaking in the art, his words, his name on the label on the wall.

I climb downstairs, take my seat in the dim-lit auditorium, look toward the stage, see the curl of his bass, the slick-down curls of his own head, still wet from the shower after rowing.

I lock my eyes on his silhouette in the darkness, as the stage lights come up from behind, as I study that head that I have held, have known, since the hour when I reached for him, newborn, and took him in my arms.

Nearly eighteen years I have loved him more than anything, have been a player in the story of his life. Have known the scenes, most every one. And now, the ones I enter into, I hold on to in my mind, in my heart, as I commit to memory, yes, but even more to soul, the whole of this chapter of mothering. Of being the moon to his orbit, his everyday rotation.

I hear the drumbeat in the background. Soft at first, muffled, but getting louder by the day. As if the dial's being turned.

The last this. The senior that. Final season.

Two months and two weeks until graduation. All around me, high school swirls. He swirls. My firstborn, love of my life.

I pore over each and every frame. Take time. Stop, in mid conversation, as he lies, stretched out at the end of a long day, reaches for my popcorn, tells me silly stories. I stop and marvel. Take in each syllable, but witness, too, the quirks and gestures I have known for so many years. The way he taps his thumb, crosses his leg, and kicks his foot.

I marvel at the mere fact that at the end of these long days we untwine together, I am hearing in real time, without phone line or typed e-mail. I can, for a few more short months, take in his life in 3-D, full-plane topography.

And so, as if storing for the future, for the days when he won't be here, won't be coming home soon, for the days when I ache to see his shining eyes, when I'll give anything for a jumbled pair of sweaty socks to be dropped across his room…

I am gathering the frames, the moments of his wholeness, one facet at a time. I am doing what we do when someone we love is leaving, and we are making room inside our hearts to store the memories, the sense, the wholeness.

I am holding on to time as I feel it slipping through my fingers. I am scaffolding my heart for when it's aching and these days are no longer…

From the Cookery Files...

When you're thinking ahead to the dinners that won't be, and not too long from now the table will be set minus one, and you feel the sudden and irresistible urge to pull out all the stops for one sweet finale...

Shortcake Season

It must be the sunlight. Or something in the air. Or somewhere deep inside me where there's some sort of trigger. The little cord that tugs when I walk into the grocery store on a fine summer's day and spy a peach.

Not just any peach. A peach nearly garnet red, and just soft enough so when I pick it up to give a gentle squeeze, the evidence is left behind. Little indents that match precisely the tips of my fat fingers. Little indents that would mark me guilty, should the produce man ever haul me in a lineup to determine who's been doing all the groping of the soft-fleshed summer fruit.

Or better yet, when I saunter by the stand at the farmers market and eye the little balsa-wood baskets of orchard-plucked peaches. Lined up all in a row, offering their fuzz and their flesh to the cause.

The cause, of course, is shortcake. 'Tis the season for the shortest cakes I know.

Those bumpy, golden squats of cloudlike dough. Cumulus, a whole sky full, lined up on a baking sheet, if I've been lazy and not used a biscuit cutter. Or scalloped round and uniform, the effervescence arising in puffy tops, if I've *not* been lazy, if I've followed shortcake etiquette and unearthed the cutter from the bottom of the baking drawer.

I learned these things—the easy way and, alternately, the proper way to form a shortcake—at the sturdy elbow of my mother's mother, Lucille, otherwise known as Oma. She was the only grandmama I ever got to cook beside, in the steamy Cincinnati kitchen where she was undisputed queen in that burg they call the Queen City.

I can see her now, sifting flour, cutting butter, making pea-sized grains of flour-butter dough bits. But I cannot see closely enough to know if it's one stick or two of butter, and a cup or a cup-and-a-half of sifted flour. I have no clue what else might be in her mix, her magic potion.

Alas, my dilemma: I fully hear the call of the shortcake, but I've no clear route to get there.

I thought about winging it, but that could lead to leaden clouds. And what I'm after is cumulus congestus, the loftiest of all.[4]

So I abandoned Lucille and her hand-me-down tin of well-worn, butter-smeared "What's Cookin'?" recipe cards, where I'd not found a single one labeled "Mama Lu's Shortcake." Instead I turned to *The Silver Palate Cookbook*, where the pair of Rosso and Lukins awaited, twiddling their buttered thumbs, wondering why I'd not wandered by sooner.[5]

Sure enough, they do not leave me without a path to puffy clouds. Right there, spilling across pages 276 and 277, they tell me just what I need to catch me a shortcake cloud on short notice.

Height-of-Summer Peach Shortcake

Provenance: *Julee Rosso and Sheila Lukins,* The Silver Palate Cookbook + *my grandma, Lucille Glaser*

Yield: 6 shortcakes

6 cups sliced peaches (or any soft-fleshed fruit you choose—
 strawberries, the classic)
2 teaspoons lemon juice, fresh squeezed
½ cup brown sugar
2 cups unbleached all-purpose flour
2 tablespoons white sugar
¾ teaspoon salt
1 tablespoon baking powder

4 tablespoons unsalted butter, chilled
½ cup light cream
2 tablespoons unsalted butter, softened, for topping
1½ cups heavy cream, chilled
a few sprigs of mint

Preheat oven to 450 degrees Fahrenheit.

Rinse and slice peaches (peel if you choose; I don't). Tumble into a bowl. Add lemon juice and brown sugar, stir, and set aside. If you won't be assembling shortcakes for a few hours, you'll want to tuck the peach bowl into the fridge. What you're after is the peachy-sugary syrup in which those slices will bathe.

Sift flour, white sugar, salt, and baking powder together in a mixing bowl.

Cut in 4 tablespoons chilled butter until mixture resembles oats. Pour in cream and mix gently until just blended.

Roll dough onto floured work surface to a thickness of ⅝ inch. (For heaven's sake, they expect a ruler here.) Cut into 3-inch circles with cookie cutter (or upside-down juice glass, if you are my Grandma Lucille). Gather scraps, roll again, and cut more rounds; you should have six rounds. (Alternately: to make drop [or lazy] biscuits, use an additional ¼ cup cream and drop the dough by large spoonfuls onto greased baking sheet.)

Bake shortcakes on greased baking sheet for about 10 minutes, or until puffed and lightly browned.

Cool the biscuits slightly, split them, and spread softened butter lightly over the cut surfaces. Set the bottoms on dessert plates, spoon on sliced peaches, and crown with the tops of the biscuits. Whip chilled cream and spoon a dollop onto each shortcake. Adorn with a pinch of fresh mint. Ferry to the table, or summer porch, channeling the grandma who inspired you so long ago.

Fledgling: Taking Flight

fledgling: *(n.)* *(also fledgeling)*, 1846, as a noun meaning "young bird" (one newly fledged); from *fledge* + diminutive suffix *-ling*.

fledge: *(v.)* "to acquire feathers," 1560s, from Old English adjective *flycge* (Kentish *flecge*; in *unfligge* "featherless," glossing Latin *implumes*) "having the feathers developed, fit to fly," from Proto-Germanic *flugja-* "ready to fly" (cognates: Middle Dutch *vlugge*, Low German *flügge*), from Proto-Indo-European *pleuk-* "to fly." Meaning "bring up a bird" (until it can fly on its own) is from 1580s.[1]

"A young bird that has grown enough to acquire its initial flight feathers and is preparing to leave the nest." The fledgling phase lasts from the time the young leave the nest until they are no longer dependent upon the parents for food.[2]

Taped, All Right

On Surrendering to Faith

*Y*ou would have thought it was an instrument for which I needed a license, the way I wielded it, the way I darn-near steamrolled whatever got in my way. Stand back, was the only word of caution uttered.

I had my hands on a certified defense weapon, with sticky side.

All it was, was a roll of Scotch shipping tape. Heavy duty, specified. I made sure I got the strongest one known to humankind.

I'd bought two rolls (can never have too much). Weeks ago. Had let them idle beside the pile of dorm essentials tucked in the living room corner, the pile I tried to pretend was not there.

I knew that someday soon the hour would come when it was time to turn the flattened cardboard boxes back into three-dimensional pop-up vessels. When the fallen trees would be called upon to do their duty: to get my firstborn's college must-haves—the memory-foam mattress topper, the shower caddy, the over-the-door towel rods, the extra-long twin sheets—to the room where they'd be home.

So there I was, alone in the living room, when at last I lifted the gizmo that spits out the tape. It's heavy. It's plastic handled. It's got one sharp cutting edge that can rip the dickens out of your lowly mortal flesh.

I started strapping strips of tape. It hit me right away: I liked the feel of all that sticky, gooey plastic holding in the contents of my firstborn's brand-new life. I strapped and strapped. Cut nice, long slabs of tape. Slapped 'em, sealed 'em, ran my palms smooth along the not-sticky side.

Suddenly I realized I was taping as if there were no tomorrow. I must have used half a roll of tape. On the first box.

Then I got to the second. Was overcome with the need to tuck in one last love note.

Hope that strapping six-foot-something lad doesn't mind that I grabbed a sheet of construction paper. Pink construction paper. And with my favorite zigzag scissors, I cut out a little pink heart. Wrote, in red, "forever my beloved." Or some such words. It's all a blur now. I was in a fevered, sticky-taped frenzy when I did it.

All I knew was that suddenly I was aswirl in out-of-body incantation. I was taping each and every box as if mere Scotch tape could keep my boy from harm. From any harm.

I wasn't so much taping to keep the boxes from splitting in the UPS truck. I was taping to keep my boy safe on the side of the mountain he'll climb during freshman orientation. I was taping to give him strength on the all-nighters I know he'll pull. I was taping to avert the stern glance of some professor who might tell my boy a thing or two about the responsibilities of scholarship, should he dare to blow a due date on some ninety-page thesis.

I was taping against the heartache that will come if someday he loves someone who doesn't love him back. I was taping to keep him afloat in all the rivers, in all the boats, that he will row.

And that's when I realized, once again, that motherprayer is so much more than words. It's what we do and breathe.

It's stirring oatmeal on a winter's morning, it's using half a roll of tape to seal shut, to protect, a box of sundries for a college dorm room, as if in simple acts of stirring, sealing, we can wrap our children—even when they're no longer little ones—in a sacred shield of holy light.

Impenetrable, we pray. "Be safe," the final words we whisper every time. Words that, now, mean so much more than simply, "I love you." That's understood, implicit.

"Be safe" is poetry, is vessel, for "I would die if you were hurt, were harmed."

"Be safe" is motherprayer for when you send your child, the fruit of your womb quite frankly, off into the world, a world you can't control, a world that some days, some dark hours, shatters you.

"Be safe" is hope and faith boiled down into two short syllables. "Be safe" is the last line of defense, the thin membrane on the other side of which prayer and holy angels pick up the load.

And some late-summer afternoons, when the sun slants in the front-room windows, illuminating your task as you tape and seal five boxes, there are no words.

Only the mad wrapping of a mother who will not let harm come to her child—nor his memory-foam mattress topper.

So help her, God.

Learning Long Distance

On Being Lost and Finding Our Way

*I*t is as if someone turned out the lights, left me in a room, and told me to find my way out. Only, they littered the path with chairs that were tipped and piles of clothes and all sorts of stuff that grabbed at my ankles.

And before I could grope through the dark, I had to plop down in front of a box with dials and knobs and whatchamahoojies and try ever so hard to recalibrate, to find the fine balance, the delicate line, between that place where the signal has always been clear, been robust, and the newfound somewhere I've never been before: the place where I mother from afar.

And thank God almighty that this particular gymnastic act—the redefining of my place in the life of my faraway boy—is one that comes with a trapeze, the safety net of human understanding and forgiveness, and efforts, again and again, to get it right.

So far, it's been bumpy. On my end, I mean. I've klonked into chairs, tripped over clothes. Can't quite find that fine line where my own brand of embracing meets up with the newfound insistence—his insistence, that is— that the boy live his own life, spread his own wings.

And sometimes it catches me chuckling. (Truth be told, sometimes it finds me in tears.)

Let's try a tale from the light-note department (or else I'll be sniffling again): the other noontime, for instance, on what was for my boy the first day of classes.

As I am wont to do on such an occasion, I felt the magnetic pull of the wide rows of candles, the ones tucked into a cove in any Catholic church. The ones guaranteed to yank God by the sleeve and get the Holy One's wide-eyed attention. Or so I've believed forever and ever.

In this case, it was the big downtown cathedral that whispered my name, barely a mile from the place where I type. So I up and departed my typing desk, wandered through the big city, down the leafy side streets, and up through the quarter-ton doors that harbor the chamber where the cardinal and his flock kneel down to pray.

I looked and looked and could not find the single place in any church that deeply stirs my soul: the vigil lights, the prayer candles, straight, tidy rows of beeswax votives all queued up beside the offerings box. The place where, with the flick of a match, you strike your intentions and watch the smoke and the prayer rise heavenward.

Only there were no candles in the cathedral. None that I could find in any nook or cranny. So I headed to the back where the man in the uniform sat. I asked if perhaps they'd done away with old-fashioned vigil lights. He uttered not a word, pointed down the nearby stairs.

In the basement? I thought. In the catacombs of the cathedral?

Not one to argue, certainly not in a church, I did as instructed (even if the instructions came without words) and down I tiptoed, wary of what I might find at the bottom.

Lo and behold, the shiny stand of candles stood. Only they weren't candles. And there were no matches. This was, after all, the big bad city, and you can't leave a match unattended. Not in the cellar of a church that once suffered a terrible fire.

And so I did what a postmillennial mama would do. I plunked in a coin, clicked the switch and on popped that battery-operated prayer candle. And, as long as I was going high tech (and as long as I was alone, down there in the cardinal's prayer pit), I figured I ought to yank out my smartphone, that squat black box I barely know how to work. I fumbled until I found the camera icon. Then I clicked and captured the prayer-wafting bulb. As long as I was zipping along the cyber-highway, I figured, I might as well send this snapshot off to the boy at the college. So I did, with a note informing him that as long as the so-called candle was hidden away in his cell phone, we ought to consider the prayers on active duty.

I laughed as I launched my long-distance prayer light. Felt just a wee bit proud of my capacity to bend to circumstances, to adapt. To carry on as I always have. Only across time zones, mountain ranges, and ZIP codes.

But the big gulp is this: the boy is too busy, too deep into college, to let me know if my high-pixel prayer card ever plopped into his phone. (Alas, that radio silence has been the case for the whole of the last two weeks, ever since we left him on the New England green. Which I'm trying so very hard to absorb, to roll with, to not allow to eat me alive.)

So I find myself feeling a bit like a schoolgirl, one with a bit of a sweet spot for a boy who's not paying attention. Suddenly, out of the blue, I'm not sure what to say. How often to say it. Yet, I'm not inclined—never have been—to play coy. Certainly not with this child I bore, this child I love more than life.

But, right in here, I'm so downright uncertain. So not wanting to intrude. To ask too much. To bother.

This room that I'm in, it's plenty dark. And I find that I'm tripping all over the place.

I am certain, I am, that I'll find my new rhythm. But right now, right in here, I am learning long distance. And it is the most uncomfortable patch I've known in some time.

Welcome Home, College Freshman. XOXO

On Sweet and Long-Awaited Reunion

I've been imagining the sound for months: his footsteps.

The house has been hollow without them, the thud I came to know as his as he stumbled out of the bed and galloped down the stairs.

I can almost feel the gust of the wind as the front door swings open and in pops that curly-haired mop I last buried my nose in on a hot August day when I left him on a leafy college quad a thousand miles away.

But any day now—I could tell you the hours and minutes—we are about to fall into the sweetest of homecomings, the freshman in college coming home for the very first time.

It's a film loop I've played in my mind over and over. Since way back before he was gone. It was, in many ways, a salve to the wound that was growing, deepening as the day of his leaving finally arrived. Nearly swallowed me whole, that widening gash.

I've long savored the romance of November, when the light turns molasses, the air crisp, and planes fill the sky, the crisscrossing of hearts headed home. But never before had I felt it so deeply.

This year, one of those jets is carrying home my firstborn.

Now, all these months later, I can only imagine the boy who's more of a man now. Calls home just once a week, Sundays, after 5 p.m. "Circa 1975," I call it, just like when I was a freshman in college and had to wait for the rates to go down to report in to the grown-ups back home.

It took me the better part of a month to get used to the missing sounds in our house. To not wince each night when I laid down three forks, not four. To not leave on the porch light as I climbed up to bed.

Over the months, I've learned to steer clear of particular shelves in the grocery store, because they hold his favorites—the turkey jerky, the sharp cheddar, stuff I used to grab without thinking, his stuff.

Curiously, I haven't spent much time in his room. Except once, when I tackled the closet, folded every last T-shirt, rolled up loose socks, rubbing my hand over the cloth, absorbing the altered equation, that I was now the mother of a faraway child.

And so, I'm looking forward to when the place at the kitchen table will be ours again, the place where we talked until the wee hours, poring over the landscape of his life, refining the art of listening, asking just the right questions.

I leapt out of bed days ago, scribbled a list of all the foods I wanted to buy, to tuck on the pantry shelves, to pack in the fridge. I flipped open a cookbook to a much-spattered page, the recipe for one of his favorites. It's as if the alchemy of the kitchen will fill places that words cannot.

I can barely contain the tingling that comes with knowing that, any day, he'll be boarding a plane, crossing the sky, putting his hand on the knob on our door.

My beautiful boy, the boy I've missed more than I will ever let on, he's coming home to the house that's been aching to hear him again.[3]

Never Enough

On the Insatiable Nature of Motherlove

I should have mastered this. Should have figured this out. Should have, should have, should have.

But I haven't.

Not when it comes to saying goodbye, not when the goodbye is to my firstborn, grand thump in my heart, big brother to the little guy, my firstborn who's been off at college for nearly three semesters now.

You'd think I could get through it without the preamble rumble in my belly, without the pounding in my heart, without the tears welling and spilling.

But I haven't.

Each time, I swear, it feels as though someone is unplugging a cord that keeps my glow up and glowing. That has something to do with how I breathe. That puts the hum in my heart.

Each time, in the hours before he leaves again for school, as I start to feel the yanking, the turning and twisting of parts deep inside, as I start to picture the hours and days ahead without him, without the uncoiling of conversation that comes, unexpected, as I chop in the kitchen, as I fold laundry, as I tie my shoes and head out for a stroll, I start to see the color draining away.

I start to feel empty all over again.

I think back to the days of long-ago villages, when a mother and son would never be farther than a few cottages apart, down behind a waist-high stone wall, through an arched timbered doorway, in a room where embers on the hearth burned orange, persimmon, and red. (I've always been a fool for storybook pictures.)

I wonder why, nowadays, mothers and children need to live miles and miles, whole time zones, apart.

Oh, of course, I settle back into my rhythms. Get used to plowing through the day without the flash of his million-watt smile. Without dinners fueled by his stories. (Fact is, I don't mind, not one little bit, seeing his bunk smooth and unrumpled. Don't miss the volcano of clothes he spills on the bedroom floor.)

We left the boy back in New York City. He's a man now. My last glimpse of him was under a streetlight at Ninety-Fourth and Lexington. He filled out his Shetland sweater, his chest now strikingly, breathtakingly, the shape and size and heft of my own papa's. A chest I always loved. A chest that made me feel safe against the world. And now that chest belongs to my son, my sweet boy, my strapping six-foot-three chunk of a man.

As I stepped back from his hug, from his long arms, broad shoulders, soft hands, I felt the pull like stretching of dough. I, into the distance. He, into the thick of his life. A whole weekend before him, a weekend romping with his beloved cousin and aunt through the best of New York, a New York I'll never see.

Fact is, it's his life he lives now. Whole chapters and verse distant to me. Unknown. Uncharted.

As it should be. As it's meant to be.

But that does not make the parting of mother and child one drop easier. Not for this mother anyway.

It's not that I want him tucked by my side. God, no. This is why and how I've raised him—to spread his arms wide as wide can be, to wrap in as much and as deep as he can, and then to soar high.

It's just that along with that soaring comes the fact that mama bird's back in the nest, or up on some other limb, watching the sky, watching the loop-de-loops. Wings on alert, ready to spread, to enfold, in case there's a fall, a need to harbor, to shelter again.

And that airspace between mother and child, that life space, it just seems to take—every time—getting used to.

I always think, I've never my fill of him. Never enough of his stories. Never enough of his heart.

Never, ever enough.

Why We Do It

On Falling in Love and Never Looking Back

I'd just pulled the sheets up toward my nose when, from the far end of the house, the ring rang. The little guy, from his bed across the hall, announced: "Mom, your phone's ringing." I mumbled back, "I'm asleep. I don't answer phones at all hours of the night."

Then the old black phone beside our bed rang. This time we answered.

It was the college kid. And at ten o'clock on a Sunday night, he decided he wanted to talk. Needed to, is what it amounted to. So for most of an hour I lay there, flat on my back, holding the phone to my ear until wrists and elbows got stiff and achy, so I'd rearrange the cradling of the little black box that connected me and my faraway boy.

After a while I started to notice that the sleeping lump beside me was doing just that: sleeping (or trying to, anyway). So I flipped back the sheets, hauled my tired self out of bed, and spent the next good hour curled in a chair in the college kid's room, where he and I wound to the end of the list—the things that must be discussed at midnight on Sunday, at the end of a very long weekend, after a very long week.

It's why I call this the most important job I will ever do.

It's why, two days later, when I went to visit a dear, dear friend who's just had a baby, her first, I marveled as I watched her besotted with her sweet breathing, gurgling, occasionally squeaking ten-day-old. I saw that look in her eyes. I felt the wonderment. I recognized right away how, suddenly, this little nine-pound wad of hunger and doze, it consumes you. You might keep charts of which breast is on tap and for how many minutes the little guy sucked. Back in the day, I did so with paper and pen and a safety pin I tried to remember to move from one nursing bra strap to the other; my dear friend clicked her uber-smart phone, and there the breast-feeding app kept time for her, tracked which side was which and how long he was at it, the guzzler.

In that glorious meld of weaving her old life into her new one, I smiled as I looked at the piles there on her bed. She was propped up with pillows, the baby reclined on the niftiest nursing contraption I'd ever seen (looked not unlike a lifesaving flotation device, except one with a pocket for tissues and a strap for a Binky, I guess, all wrapped in quaint baby cloth). But all around her were the sorts of deep reads for which my friend lives. She'd been reading aloud pages of the *Atlantic* and *Road Song*, Natalie Kusz's heart-wrenching nonfiction tale of trauma and loss and redemption, because what newborn baby isn't lulled by the sounds of his mama's voice, and why not start the literary steeping on day one of his life?

I stayed as long as I could, till the light from the west slanted in, slanted down, slanted thinner. Watching her, listening to her and her husband recount twist after turn in her thirty-eight-hour labor, I couldn't help but be lulled back in time to the start of this ancient and timeless arc, the whole-body immersion into motherhood.

By miracle of accumulated years, I suddenly found myself twenty years away from my start. And thus, whirling inside me, I had the breathtaking knowledge of why those first hours and days are so vitally sealed. Why, as mothers, we practically need to be vacuum-swooped down the vast and cavernous tunnel of love that is the adventure of a lifetime, that is cradling a life, soon taking it by the hand and eventually letting it go, to soar and to dip and to dive all on its own. And to be there, on the end of the line, when the ring rings at ten in the night. Or eleven. Or one. Or beyond.

To fall madly in love, to feel fingers the size of a matchstick curl and cling to your flesh, to come to know the particular snorts and grunts of that loaf of blanket and fuzz strapped across your chest, across the place where your hearts pound in echo. To spend your waking hours clocking newborn input and output, it is all a part of the alchemy that seals mother to child. And keeps us in for the long haul.

What else could so fixate us, could so call out to that seed buried deep in our hearts, the one that's been waiting—at least for some of us—since the day we were born, we were cradled, to turn and do the same, to return the grace of generation upon generation? To mother a child through all the tight spots and twists that tumble onto the miles and miles from nursing pillow to college diploma, and each day ever after?

If it weren't for hearts hermetically sealed from the get-go, how else could we stick with this uncharted program? Who'd sign up for a road trip that, at any turn, might find you splayed on the bathroom floor at three in the morning when a little guy is retching his guts out, or when the bath needs to be drawn while the birds warble their morning song because the mercury on the thermometer reads 105 and you're scared out of your wits and willing yourself not to crumble?

What else would keep you upright when the phone rings and the next thing you know, strangers are talking of airlifts and ambulances and necks that are broken in multiple places? Or keep your knees from buckling when your lanky kid is lying there in the ICU half-buried under a web of IV tubes and oxygen lines running this way and that, and you count as many as six different needles shoved under the skin of his banged-up and bleeding forearms?

Motherhood is not for the faint of heart, and the heart needs to triple in size, so it seems, to pack in the requisite vast and infinite wisdom— and patience and sheer calculation and imagination and stamina and worry and second-guessing and, yes, full-throttle pangs of remorse when we get it wrong, time after time.

And motherhood holds no escape clause. We're in it for keeps. Which is why we sometimes find ourselves mumbling aloud, as we shake a fist to the heavens and ask why-oh-why we are once again searching the house for the shoe/the soccer ball/the library book that somehow escaped from its last known location. Or driving umpteen hundred miles to drop off a precious load at some far-flung soccer field. Or sending a note to the teacher asking if maybe we could meet after school to find out why this fourth-grade math is so very mind-bending.

But what other adventure known to humankind might find you taking a little child by the hand, just after a soggy afternoon's rain, and heading out the door in search of worms that might need rescue, plucked from the unforgiving concrete sidewalk and tenderly placed in the oozy garden? Or have you witnessing, from the very front row, the moment when mixed-up alphabet letters on a page suddenly rearrange themselves into equations called words, and the child is off and reading?

Oh, it takes love, all right. Deep-veined love. The sort that reroutes all the wires inside you. That literally re-scripts your dreams, gives center stage to the newest, dearest soul in your life, one you suddenly realize you can't live without. And for the first time ever, perhaps, you know that you'd throw yourself, in an instant, before a car or a train or a boulder barreling toward that babe who looks in your eyes as if his life depends on you.

Because, truly, it does.

From the Cookery Files...

When you're about to welcome home your far-flung child, or anyone you love, and you want the whole kitchen bewitched by the heavenly vapors that rise from a long, slow oven. And if you're a believer, besides, in the lung-filling embrace that begins the instant the door's cracked ajar, before you even wrap your arms round the shoulders you've so longed to squeeze with all your might...

It's Brisket Weather

Borrowing amply from Truman Capote, who in his delicious and utterly memorizable 1956 treasure, *A Christmas Memory*, tells us of his eccentric sixty-something-year-old cousin who presses her nose to the kitchen window, gauges the Novemberness of the outside tableau, and exclaims, "Oh my, it's fruitcake weather!...Fetch our buggy. Help me find my hat."

At our house, I have been known to wake up, sniff the air, and proclaim, "It's brisket weather." Whether autumn or spring, the in-between seasons, or even deepest of winter; doesn't matter at our house. We invent reasons for brisket—or my boys do, anyway. And so it was the other day, as I trotted off to the butcher who had cleaved and wrapped seven and a half pounds of pure red steer, laced heavily with adipose. As he hoisted the slab from the cooler, he glanced at the name—*Mahany*—scrawled on the whitepaper-wrapped log. Then, impishly, he raised one eyebrow and inquired, "That Jewish?" Well, no, Mister Meat Man. But my husband is, our boys are half-and-half, Jewish and Catholic, and we grab at any excuse for brisket, be it Hanukkah (the Jewish wintertime Festival of Lights) or Pesach (springtime's retelling of the Exodus story) or whenever a kid wings his way home from college.

One of the curious things about being an Irish Catholic mother in a

Motherprayer

Jewish-Catholic family is that you have no long lineage of Jewish ancestral recipes you call your own. You have, in fact, something far better: an amalgam of adopted Jewish mothers and the best of their best. I've got Ina's matzo balls; Aunt Joni's tips on storing, freezing, and reheating latkes; Liat's hamantaschen; and Audrey's tzimmes with potato kugel topping, that last one cut from the *Los Angeles Times*, now yellowed, and long ago scribbled with Audrey's thoughts on how to improve it.

Brisket I've got in triplicate, and the one I turn to—time after time, for holidays or homecomings—is the one I now call my.own, although it came from a friend's mother, a mother I've met only once, at the side of a pool at a seven-year-old's birthday splash long long ago, where the meeting was doused liberally in chlorinated pool water. But once or twice or thrice a year, my friend's mama and I, we make brisket together—in that way that a hand-me-down recipe stirs kinship to life. Alone in my kitchen, I listen closely as Mrs. Ellin insists it must be Heinz Chili Sauce and nobody else's. Dare not deviate as she guides me through the rinsing and patting dry of the beef slab.

And then it's into the vault of the oven, where the heat has its way, coaxes surrender of sinew and spice. It never takes long, as my friend's mama has promised, till my kitchen is filled with celestial aroma: all chili sauce, red wine, cloves, and pungent drift of bay leaves.

All the while, we are whispering prayers, Jewish and Catholic, for fork-tender, melt-in-your-mouth, mind-if-I-help-myself-to-more. We'll let you know if our brisket prayers are answered.

Welcome–
Home
Brisket

Provenance: Harlene Ellin's mom, whose prescription I follow religiously

Yield: Depends on how hungry you are, but you'd be safe to guess this will feed 6

3 pounds first-cut brisket (Such things a Catholic girl must
    learn; who knew from first-, second-, or even third-cut?)
1 cup Heinz Chili Sauce*
½ cup brown sugar
¼ cup dry red wine*
¼ cup water
1 small or medium onion, sliced
3 cloves, whole

6 black peppercorns, whole
3 bay leaves

* If you're making this Kosher for Passover, you'll need to swap Kosher-for-Passover ketchup for the chili sauce (for zing, add ¼ teaspoon garlic powder, ¼ teaspoon onion powder, and ½ teaspoon chili powder) and be sure to use Kosher-for-Passover wine.

Rinse brisket and pat dry with paper towels. Preheat oven to 325 degrees Fahrenheit. In a small bowl combine chili sauce, brown sugar, wine, and water. Mix well. Pour ¼ of chili sauce mixture into a roasting pan. Place brisket on sauce, fat side up. Place onions, cloves, peppercorns, and bay leaves evenly over brisket. Top with remaining chili sauce mixture.

Cover roasting pan tightly. Bake brisket for 50 to 55 minutes per pound, or until meat is fork tender. (Pay attention to the math, friends; it makes for a long, slow roasting. A 3-pound brisket will roast for at least 2½ hours.)

Remove meat from pan and place it in a container. Remove bay leaves, peppercorns, and cloves from gravy, and put gravy in another container. Refrigerate meat and gravy, separately, for several hours or overnight.

To reheat brisket, slice against the grain to desired thickness and place in a covered casserole dish sprayed with cooking-oil spray. Remove and discard any congealed fat from gravy. Pour the gravy over the meat. Cover and reheat in a 375-degree-Fahrenheit oven for 30 minutes or until heated through. (Brisket can be reheated in a microwave.) In a word: mmmm.

Almost Empty Nest

Incubation and hatching: Whether eggs in a single clutch will hatch simultaneously or sequentially over an extended period of time is determined by the onset of incubation. In many birds...incubation does not begin until the last egg has been laid....In contrast, many other birds begin incubation prior to the laying of the last egg of the clutch. This results in asynchronous hatchings separated by anywhere from a few hours to several days, depending on how soon incubation commences following the start of egg laying.[1]

—*The Birder's Handbook: A Field Guide to the Natural History of North American Birds*

Joy of One

On Lavishing Love, Without Apology

Sooner or later, it happens. To anyone who's assembled a tumbled lot of kids. Housed them. Fed them. Worried through a night or two.

It's the law of simple arithmetic. Subtraction, actually.

$x - 1$ (the basic equation, if x is greater than 1, and if applied in serial countdown) eventually $= 1$.

For all the momentum you'd once acquired under that one shingled roof, for all the noise once collected over forks and spoons and spilled milk, there comes a day when there's only one poor child under your sights.

Poor child, indeed.

That one and only kid is unshakably under the steady gaze of eyes that have no distraction, that aren't too often pulled hither or yon.

That poor kid is all alone in the glare of your watchtower.

And in our house, the grown-ups come in pairs. So, in fact, he's under double glare.

He wakes up some fine mornings to not one but two tall people tickling him from slumber. One's armed with warm, moist washcloth (the Turkish spa treatment, you might rightly think). The other employs soft circles to the hollow between the bumps where angel wings were supposed to sprout.

He saunters downstairs to made-to-order pancakes and bacon. On mornings like this, when all that slumber was hard to shake, one of the tall people caves and offers a ride in the little black sedan. Complete with

Motherprayer

concentrated conversation, the rare sort that comes when the interviewer is truly, deeply interested in all that lurks deep inside your soul.

Now, you might be retching right about here. Thinking, holy smokes, what sort of overindulgent parenting is this? Where's the rough-and-tough school of hit the Eject button, hightail 'em out the door, stuff a granola bar in their pocket, and kick 'em in the pants, with a casual, "Have a good one," tossed over your shoulder as you slam the door behind?

Well, there are rare few chances in this board game called A Life in which to pull out all the stops, to give it everything you've got, to score one more chance to do it right, to love with all your heart.

So that seems to be the MO over here.

By accident of gestational bumps and broken hearts, we're in our third chapter of parenting. We had the One-and-Only Round One (a round we thought would never end), the Oh My Gosh It's Two (a round it *seemed* would never end), and now, thanks to a very faraway college quad, we've got One and Mostly Only.

Day in and day out, it's a ratio of two to one.

And perhaps the most beautiful part of being the mama of a twelve-year-old when you yourself are fifty-six, barreling toward fifty-seven, is that you are wise enough to know: there is no more sacred incubator in this blessed gift of life than the one into which you pour your heart and whatever accumulated wisdom you've scraped up along the way—that holy vessel called a growing, stretching child.

Doesn't matter to me if the child comes by birth or by heart, or simply wanders down the sidewalk and finds a place on my couch. It's a nasty speed-chase out there, with cars flying into ditches right and left. If the walls within which I dwell happen to offer rare respite, time out, breathing room, a place where dreams can be launched and hurts aired out to dry, well then I'm posting a shingle on my doorpost: "Time out offered here."

Even after all these days—and there've been 4,420—since that sweet boy landed in my arms, I consider it a miracle of the first order that he's here at all. Never mind that mop of curls. Or the bottomless smile and the matching dimples. Or the tender way he takes my hand and gives it a squeeze in the middle of driving from anywhere to anywhere. Never mind that, mid-lope out the door, he hits the brakes and circles back for a goodbye hug—one for each grown-up.

166

Never mind all that.

It's just the rare, precious miracle of the chance to rocket-launch one more sack of hopes and dreams and heart. To try to pack in all the love and goodness and tender toughness that just might add a shard of light to this sometimes darkening planet.

I've always said he seems to know, deep inside his soul, that he was a last-chance baby. The one who beat the odds. The one who left his mama jaw-dropped and quaking at the news. Those sterile hens in the Bible—Sarah (ninety when she birthed Isaac), Rebekah, and Rachel, to name a few of the so-called barren—had nothing on me when it came to being flabbergasted at the revelation (although my shriek came upon seeing the little pregnancy plus sign turn pink, which I don't think was part of the biblical story).

So he seems to indulge us in our overlavishing. Fear not, we try to keep it in check. At least when anyone's watching. But I happen to have married my teacher in the Tenderness Department. In patience, too. That man has never once uttered a note in the tone of shrill, a tone I know by heart. Used to be I didn't stop myself until he shot me a withering glance. That stopped me, rattled me back on track.

But over all these years—and there've been twenty so far in the parenting corral—I've learned to take his lead and not auto-leap—well, not every time—into the role of Mrs. Harsh and Overhurried.

Once upon a time, you would've thought the world depended on our getting to the nursery school on time. And I still have trouble reminding myself that a tornado-strewn whirl of clothes heaped on the bedroom floor is *not* the moral equivalent of hauling swine flu into the country, hidden in a clandestine stick of salami.

I think often—expend a bumper crop of brain cells—on the subject of growing kids. It's religion to me, the holiest sort. It matters more than anything else I will ever do. Closest thing to curing cancer. Because it boils down to taking the heart and soul you've been handed and tenderly, wisely filling both with light. Considering them stealth missiles of planetary illumination. The answers to a Peace Prize prayer.

Oh sure, the darkness will come. We can't keep that at bay. But we can give the gift of buoyancy. We can keep the boing in the human spirit. The bounce-back machine that takes the wallops and rights itself again.

Motherprayer

There's not a creature on the globe who wouldn't pray to be loved deep and pure and forever after. It's the highest hope of all creation.

And at our house he only wishes for someone else to please steal our attention. Especially when we double-team the launching him from bed.

Turning Twenty-One: A Mother Was Born

On a Birthing Deep Inside

Nothing had ever—has ever—so deeply captured my attention. You can see it in the gaze in one of the very first snapshots, the one just before we went home from the hospital, eyes locked between mother and child. You can see it in the parted lips, my lips, can almost hear the gushing in of breath, of pure undiluted amazement.

Deep down, I think, I never really believed it would happen. Had so little faith in my body—in the flesh and bones of this well-worn vessel—I gasped when they handed me that bundle. I distinctly remember drinking in his eyes, whispering, "Hullo, my sweet, so here I am, and here you are, answer to my deepest prayers, my dreams come true beginning now." And then, before I could stop myself, I zeroed in on the thighs. The thighs, I am blessed to report, were duly "pudged," rolls of flesh and perfect fat, a fat so deliciously dimpled it nearly melted me off the birthing bed.

I'd been afraid I might grow a baby without the requisite fat. In fact, I doubted my capacities as birthing chamber all along. In one long weekend, after an early set of ultrasounds, I convinced myself my baby had no brain. All you could see inside the skull was black space, blank, black space. *Oh my God*, I thought, *they've not yet broken it to me, but I think my baby might be missing his brain.* I even called a radiologist friend—on a Sunday—to find out if he'd confirm my fear.

He confirmed it not.

And, in fact, on the sultry start-of-summer Tuesday when at last that babe was born, he was a whopping eight pounds nine ounces—a good chunk of that birth weight duly tucked in the cranial cavity, where in the years since he has solidly demonstrated that brain was right where it needed to be, doing pretty much what it was wired to do.

My beautiful boy turns twenty-one the day after tomorrow, and while my hand-penned letter to him will be deeply private, the one I'm writing here is the one in which I proclaim how very deeply his birth birthed the depths of me, allowed, at last, the core of who I dreamed I could be, who I prayed I could be, to begin to take form, to emerge in light and shadow, to rise from the gauzy netherworld, to be defined in sharp outline and tender spots, and to be forming still.

It just might be most every blessed mother's story: we stumble upon the best that we can be, sometimes, when living, breathing, squawking, ever-hungry babe is cradled in our arms. Our trembling arms, to be sure. Our arms that grow stronger, surer, over all the sagas and the chapters and the countless hours of two lives entwined.

When I think back over the twenty-one years that he and I have been essential factors in each other's equations, I stand in wide-eyed wonder. I bow down low in deepest gratitude. I wince at my mistakes, moments I'd give anything to do over. And I marvel at the times when I stepped to the edge of the precipice, mustered all my courage, and leapt—that eternal life-saving instinct nestled deep in every mother's heart, the one that propels us to put form to whatever is the holy vow we take when we're first told that life stirs within.

It's unbreakable, the mother bond. It defines our days, puts order to our must-get-done list, sets us off to the ends of the earth, if need be, in search of the essential whatever, whomever—be that the medical specialist who can peer inside a child's shattered bone or merely the USB cable that's gone missing from the kid's laptop at the very hour the paper must be printed and turned in for a full semester's credit.

And it keeps us awake, long night after long night.

We learn, once motherhood comes upon us, just how long we can go without so much as a spoonful of cereal (it took me a couple of weeks to figure out how to inhale breakfast with a baby wailing in the infant seat), and how many consecutive nights we can curl up on the bathroom floor cradling a fevered child or one who's upchucking until the wee, wee hours.

When necessary, we discover we can make the scariest of phone calls, can dial up the mother of the slumber-party bully, can look the teacher in the eye and say, "I'm sorry, I don't think you understand my kid." We can even will our knees not to buckle when the ER doctors start tossing around words like *airlift* and *cervical fracture* and *severed spinal cord*. We can make promises to God—ones we swear we'll keep—when, for longer pauses than we ever thought we could endure, we're begging to be spared a kid who can't flinch a muscle from his neck down to his fingers and his toes. (And, yes, thank God, he and we were spared.)

In rare sweet moments, we find out how it feels to catch the wind and soar. We turn and see the kid we love dashing down the block to hand a crunched-up dollar bill to the homeless guy he knows by name. We nearly fall in the river as the kid who couldn't catch a fly ball now rows mightily across the finish line. We read the words his college professors send to us in e-mails that knock us off our chairs, and leave one of us brushing away the streams of tears.

We hope, we dream, we pray. We reach down deep, deeper than we ever reached before. We listen until the birds of dawn begin to sing, if that's what it takes some long, dark, hollow nights.

We find our voice along the years. We exercise our heart. We rack our brain. We love, and love some more.

And suddenly, twenty-one years have happened. Countless picture frames loop before our eyes. Words and stories bubble up and fill page upon page. Our hearts are twenty-one times the size they used to be—at least.

We have paid most exquisite attention to each and every breath and utterance all along the way. We've driven ourselves nearly mad. We've cared beyond reason. In fact, there's little room for the rational when it comes to this particular brand of love story.

We were handed a treasure. We owe it to the treasure. We owe it to the bequeathers of the treasure.

I, for certain, was handed the treasure of my life. June 22, 1993. The day the best of me was born.

A work very much in progress. The best work in all my *oeuvre*.

Tracks to My Heart

On Childhood's Treasures, Forgotten and Found

The e-mail slipped in with no more than the ubiquitous ping. It came from my faraway brother, the one with a boy of his own now, a fine little lad rounding the bend toward two.

The e-mail couldn't have been clearer:

"Hey Babs, we are thinking of getting a train set for Milo. I recall you guys had a great Thomas Train set up. If you still have it, would you be open to our borrowing it for couple of years? I totally understand you might not want to let it go. Just wondering."

In an instant, the snapshots came streaming: My own firstborn's second birthday, a summer's day so hot and sticky he wore just a Onesie as we tip-toed down the stairs to see what the birthday fairy had tucked in the living room corner. My heart nearly burst as I handed him the very first box I'd ever gone out and bought for him. It was a box so heavy the little guy couldn't lift it. He needed his papa and me. Inside: an oval of track, wooden track; one ivy-wrapped train station; and a little blue engine named Thomas, Thomas the Tank Engine, a train who'd ascend to a starring role in the celluloid loops of one boyhood.

For years and years, the consummate posture in our house was a boy perched in a crouch, his fine little fingers curled over the spine of a train as he moved it this way and that, spinning tale after tale, spewing noise after guttural noise (for that's what trains do when they speed or they crash). One by one, we collected engines and track and bridges and tunnels. We collected stories and friendships there on the floor where the tracks morphed from circle to oval to intricate geometries that looped and ducked and rose and forked. The little TV by the kitchen table played over and over the tales of the trains of the Island of Sodor, all told in the lilting tongue of one Ringo Starr, who to these children was simply Mr. Conductor, while to his parents he was the rock star drummer, now curiously cast as trainman.

Our sweet boy loved trains more than anything. For years, we rode them cross-country, falling asleep to the sway of the bunks as we rolled through the heartland, the Hudson River Valley, or the rise of the Rockies. We drove to where we could watch the lumbering locomotives switching back and forth on the sidetracks in the yard where they were hosed down and polished. We climbed aboard on Sundays and rode up and down the el line or around the Loop, Chicago's train set for grown-ups.

More than once, our little trainman plopped his head to the pillow and drifted to dreamland clutching one of his engines. He rarely left home without his striped engineer's cap. And when he was four, and we drove to a farm to fetch a striped six-week-old kitten, our little trainman inserted "Choo-Choo" as the mewling's middle name.

One Christmas, the very same brother who now wonders if we might send our train set his way stayed up the whole night, sawing and pounding vast planes and chunks of wood, a train table with sawdust-sprinkled landscape, one that stood on four stout legs and rose to the precise height of one little boy's waist, for maximum stretch of his train-steering arms. That blessed brother's all-night labor made for a Christmas awakening never to be exceeded.

Then one day, the train table was collecting dust. The trains hadn't moved one inch in the yard. They were tumbled all in a pile and, in time, tossed in a bin and tucked at the back of the basement toy shelf.

For years now, they've cowered in the dark. Too treasured to be relegated to the attic. Too forgotten to see the light of that murky playroom downstairs.

But still, that bin holds so many sparks of a boyhood, I can nearly hear its whispers. Maybe more than anyone in the house, I'm the one still clutching the tracks and the sweet-faced engines.

Around here we believe in hand-me-downs. Not only because they stretch a dollar but also because a hand-me-down is history. Is layers of story. Of love. Is animated, even its stillness.

And so, this morning, I will sift through the train bin. I will pluck out Thomas, the blue one, and James, who is red. Edward, I recall, is the kind engine (and thus, always, my favorite). And Toby is a troublemaker. How could you not love the cast of your firstborn's childhood? How could you not treasure the trains that, often, came to dinner? Made lumps in the bed clothes? Filled little-boy pockets? Turned faucets of tears if left behind, ever?

That little trainman is far from home now, a thousand miles away from the little toy trains and their table, now disassembled. He's all grown, and he told me just last week, with a thrill in his voice, that the window of his senior-year dorm room looks out on a train track that runs through the woods of his leafy New England college.

And just a bit farther north and east, in the little town of South Portland, Maine, there is a little boy who doesn't yet go to sleep dreaming of trains. But he will. Oh, he will.

As soon as I slap the shipping tape onto the cardboard box that waits in the basement. Soon as the nice mailman scoops up the parcel and plops it onto a faraway stoop. Soon as sweet Milo crouches down in that way that boys do and curls his fingers just so, round the spine of the train. And, full steam ahead, chugs through a childhood.

Coming Home to an Empty House and Other Things That Matter

On Love's Fine-Stitched Sampler and How It Holds Us Together

I was dripping from the shower, rubbing the fluffy towel around my ears, when I heard the very last sound you want to hear at 6:15 in the morning: "R-r-r-ring, r-r-r-ring!"

The phone at this dark hour is never the Nobel Committee calling to say, "You won the prize!"

And I, being of Celtic root, always suspect disaster. "Oh no, this must be awful," I muttered with certainty, as I leapt down two steps at a time to grab the phone, to take the blow I knew must be coming.

"Good morning, good morning," came the first four words. Then my mother's voice went on to tell me this: "I've been worrying." (No news, there; she and I have a special knack in that department.) "I've been thinking about tonight, and I don't want T. coming into an empty house after soccer. I think I should skip your book thing. I would love to be there. But he shouldn't be alone when he comes home. I should be there to give him dinner, keep him company."

And in those short few words I heard, once again, love defined by my mother.

"…don't want him coming into an empty house.…He shouldn't be alone."

I added those few words to the lines already etched across my heart.

The ones that include:

"I always felt the most important job I could do was take care of the family so the rest of you could go out and change the world."

And: "Once your father died, I told God I was dedicating the rest of my life to however God needs me."

In my mother's book of life, the litany of love reads like this: clothes pulled from the dryer, folded, stacked, and delivered to your bedroom chair; hot dinner, complete with cooked frozen vegetables; houseplants given a weekly dose of fluids; children driven—without grumble—to where they need to be; soccer matches attended—even if they're in kingdom come at seven in the chilly morning.

My mother, who quietly puffs her chest at the fact that she was the only one of her circle of friends deemed worldly enough and brainy enough to date my father (by virtue of the fact that she subscribed in 1953 to *Forbes* magazine), is not one to knock you over with Pythagorean theorems or deep analysis of the threat of ISIS on the world stage. She will, however, quote you lines from Emily Dickinson or Robert Browning until you beg her to stop. And she will recount every feather she's spotted since daybreak in the boughs outside her window and at her eighteen backyard feeders (that's a tad of an exaggeration, the feeder count, but I told you I have Irish roots; embellishment is our mother tongue).

And she will quietly, wordlessly, go about the business of taking care of your house—or mine. Because to my mama it is in doing that we love.

It is in wiping dry the dishes I've left dripping in the rack. It is in ferrying her little blue plastic cooler to our front door every Tuesday, always bringing a zip-top bag of this or that, the ingredients for dinner pre-measured in her kitchen to bring to mine. She's driven 9.62 miles to mix, to stir, to crank the oven, to set the table, and not forget the salt and pepper shakers. She makes a nice hot meal, circa 1970—the prime of her cooking years when she had six hungry mouths to feed, not counting her own, of course not counting her own.

My mother is not alone in stitching the tapestry of life with *petit point*, those fine-grained stitches not grand in scale, not at all, but the very threads that hold us all together, that make our lives just a notch more beautiful, more breathable.

Talk to anyone who's dying. Listen in on what they tell you matters most: curling up with a child—and a picture book—pressed against each other's curves. Sitting one minute longer on the edge of the bed while tucking someone in at night. Spooning one extra dollop of butter in the mound of mashed potatoes. Hearing the click of the front door that signals someone's home. Catching the moonlight dapple the bedclothes.

Have you ever heard how hard the dying pray for just one more round of gathering the tiniest glories of a day?

So, last night, my mama was not in the rows of a charmed bookstore, one with paned windows and Oriental rugs and books bursting from the walls. She did not listen to her only daughter read from the pages of her just-published dream-come-true. (She's not yet been to a reading, so it's not as though she took a pass because she'd already sat there drinking it in.) No, my mama was home to turn the hall light on. To press her hand to the door handle when a tired fist knocked. She was there to warm up the orange chicken she'd made two nights before. To scoop out peas in butter sauce.

And there she sat, with the boy we all love—so he wouldn't be alone while his mama was off reading and his papa was far away gathering notes for a newspaper story.

My mama stayed home at my house because she knew—without words—that it was the purest form of love that she could ladle out for all of us—not least of all for me, always torn when pulled away from where I, too, know I most belong.

My mama, once again, taught us, with so few words, that there's no headline-grabbing heroism in a certain brand of loving. But in the end, the very end, those small acts of utter selfless majesty are the surest holy gospel we could ever know.

And it's why—to this very day—I understand so deeply that I'm most at home, most solidly rooted, when I, too, partake of the tender acts of stitching a certain kind of attention into the daily cloth of those I love so truly deeply.

As If a Dream...

On Savoring Every Succulent Moment

The last flicker of red taillight just faded from the alley. I'd pressed my cheek as close to the glass as I could press—short of stepping out into the near-frozen morning—straining to see the last dab of red glow fading away.

And, like that, poof, he's gone.

My little Christmas dream, my wish come true, has come to its hollow end. The boy I love is headed back to the college on the faraway hill, where, alone in his dorm room, the light through the window will burn. The green slope between red-brick dorms, one after another all in a square, it will be empty, will echo with the whisper of the few faint footsteps. The kid I love is among the one or two in the college who've been granted permission to type straight through the new year.

So Christmas here was cut short, cut short by a very long thesis due in two short weeks—or, as I count it, seventeen days, six hours, and nineteen minutes.

Christmas this year was condensed. Distilled to its short, sweet essence.

Which, in many ways, made it all the more delectable, all of it tumbled one delicious moment atop another. Until last night, as I was clearing the Christmas feast dishes, and the lurch in my belly made itself known. He's leaving again, I remembered. Before the dark of the dawn fades, he will be gone, I remembered.

So this morning, I did what mothers too often do: I watched the light fade away, into the too-far distance.

We wait, some sweet homecoming moments, for the light to come in through the distance. And then, on the other end of the dizzying spell of squeezing a hand that's grown far bigger than ours, and bending low for a kiss to the brow of the sleeping man who's back in his old twin bed, on the other end of shoulder pressed against shoulder at the cookstove, or plopping on the edge of each other's bed for one or two thoughts shared in the dark, there comes the hour when the light pulls away, into the darkness again.

And so, in the space in between, we immerse ourselves deep in the holiest way to live: at full and piercing attention. Stripping away the parts of ourselves that might otherwise get in our way—the parts that, say, might prefer to do things a particular way; the part that normally flinches when butter and oil are spattered all over the cookstove (and the wall and the floor), but not this hour when it's the college kid plying his craft of Brussels sprouts bathed in a sizzling skillet of garlic and fat upon fat; the part that hadn't planned on going to church on the far end of a one-hour traffic jam, but once we got there, well, I found myself awash in tears at the joy spread across the kid's face as he remembered the church where he'd made his First Holy Communion.

So it goes, when there's only so much time—and you're graced with the knowledge that, soon as it begins, it's tumbling toward the close. You shrug off all the little things that don't matter. You set your divining rod to high alert. And you whirl through the short spell—the too-short spell—of sixty-three hours and change (including sleep time) and you inhale as if through a double-wide straw.

Which, from time to time, is a very fine way to practice the art of being alive. As if the edges of your consciousness were bordered with a high-voltage fence. Where, if you drifted into unconsciousness, into not paying attention, a wee zap to the noggin would jostle you back into full-throttle live-in-the-moment.

I remember how, in the days just before our wedding, a wise someone whispered to me a trick I've tried to ply ever since, even though the original instruction was only meant to pertain to the bride's walk down the aisle: freeze-frame the moment, the wise person intoned. Take snapshots in your head, all along the way. That way you'll never forget it.

So I attempt to pull that old trick from my tool kit whenever the occasion demands. As it did this Christmas. As it did this very short spell when all I wanted was the one thing I found under the tree: both my boys, and their papa, nestled shoulder to shoulder for unbroken hours.

The little guy practically couldn't let go. We were hunkered down watching a movie, and there were the little one's arms, draped wholly across his big brother's chest. Loping down a city sidewalk, the big one flopped his very long arm down and around the little one's cap-covered, curly-haired head.

The two of them stayed up late all three nights. I drifted to sleep hearing their hilarity rise up the stairs, around the bend, and into my bed. Last night I woke up long enough to hear a line I promised myself I'd memorize, but then, darn it, I woke up and couldn't quite remember. All I know is it was something about, "You're the best brother that ever there was."

Which, really, is all I need to remember, to know.

I wished for one thing for Christmas. I wished for one thing my whole life long: that through trial and error, and stumble and fall, and mistake after blunder, I might over time figure out how to live and breathe love in a way that was purely contagious, that spread like a rash.

I wished for a womb of love, long, long ago. I prayed that the boy I was about to birth would always, always know that love was his beginning and middle and end. I've lived and breathed to untangle wires, sandpaper rough spots; to make what unfolds in this house a pure bath of tender-hearted, full-throttle kindness. With a fat dollop of joy.

And this Christmas I watched it unfold, one slow frame at a time.

I've got the whole roll cached in my heart.

From the Cookery Files...

When old-fashioned comfort food—nothing frilly or fancy or nouvelle about it—is the order of the day. When riffling through the banged-up recipe box unearths a morsel from your not-so-distant past, and a tucked-away era springs back to life as you go about your kitchen ministrations. When the whole point of dinner is simply to say, "I love you through and through."

Pause. Bow Head. Strike Sullen Pose.

"Did you see the obituaries?" my mother asked, first thing one October day in 2007. My mother was insistent, was clearly undone. "Peg died."

Peg Bracken, she meant, iconic cookbook author and midcentury humorist who penned a monthly jab at domesticity in *Family Circle* magazine. Peg, who might as well have been our next-door neighbor growing up. The one who would have passed Virginia Slims over the picket fence. Poured a cocktail as soon as the kiddies polished off their after-school snack. I'm thinking her only use for her apron was to wipe her muddy shoes.

Despite—or because of—the anarchy, my mother consulted her. Followed her. Stood off in the corner of the kitchen with her, often, snickering in a most rebellious way.

She was, apparently, my mother's alter ego. She was, maybe, the trouble-maker my mother wasn't. She was, in 1960 when her cookbook came out—her anti-cookbook, really, *The I Hate to Cook Book*—a breath of something new in the simmering winds over by the range (for what had been the stove became the range somewhere in the latter half of the last century).

Her most famous recipe, perhaps, the one uncobwebbed for all the obits, is one called "Skid Road Stroganoff."

It goes like this:

"Start cooking those noodles, first dropping a bouillon cube into the noodle water. Brown the garlic, onion, and crumbled beef in the oil. Add the flour, salt, paprika, and mushrooms, stir, and let it cook five minutes while you light a cigarette and stare sullenly at the sink."[2]

Even now, it's hard not to love a woman who whisks *sullenly* into a recipe for stroganoff.

In the house where I grew up, that blue book with the funny drawings—drawn, by the way, by Hilary Knight, who drew the daylights out of *Eloise at The Plaza*—stood mostly for one dish: a dish once named Chicken-Rice Roger. But in our house, now, it is mostly known as Chicken Rice Grammy, for it is the perfect embodiment of all things cozy in a covered dish.

It (a) comes bubbling out of the oven, (b) is made (unless you're a rule breaker) with stuff dumped from a can, and (c) is the surest cure for a bad day that I can think of.

And so, here's to Peg, now departed; Peg who made my mother giggle. Peg, who had my mama dumping cans all around the kitchen. And to my mama, who's made this more Grammy Tuesdays than I could possibly count. And never sullenly.

Chicken Rice Grammy

Provenance: Peg Bracken's The I Hate to Cook Book *(I confess to a tad of tinkering here, as I've quashed dear Peg's tin-canned fixation.)*

Yield: Serves 6, if not too hungry

4 to 6 chicken breasts, skinless and boneless, cut into halves
¾ cup uncooked rice (I opt for brown rice)
I cup mushrooms, chopped
I onion, diced
1¾ cups chicken broth
Optional: ¾ cup artichoke hearts, red pepper strips, olives,
    whatever add-ins you fancy

Preheat oven to 350 degrees Fahrenheit. Grease a 9-inch baking dish. (I use a soufflé dish.)

Brown chicken in sauté pan. Dump golden-browned chicken atop rice, mushrooms, onion, broth, and add-ins already placed in baking dish.

Bake, covered, for 1 hour. (If you're using brown rice, you might want to check at the half-hour mark and add a splash more chicken broth if needed.) As you disinter from the oven, tip your casserole lid to dear Peg, who despite her disinclination always delivered delicious.

And in the End: The Wind Beneath My Wings

How do birds fly? Everybody knows that a bird is supported in the air by its wings, but how exactly the wings performed this magic remained a mystery until the late nineteenth century.... In Newtonian terms, a flying bird is immersed in the earth's gravitational field, which exerts a force, the bird's weight, directed towards the earth's center.... A bird has to supply work at a steady rate to impart downward momentum on a stream of air. If the downwash stops, the bird falls. Power is the rate of doing work, and it is this unremitting requirement for power to support the weight that makes flight fundamentally different from other forms of locomotion.... The secret of flight, in birds and aircraft alike, is to use lift forces for supporting the weight and for manoeuvering, but to arrange that work is done against much smaller drag forces. [The central equation rests on three rudimentary measurements: mass, wing span, and wing area], unfortunately not to be found in traditional "morphometrics" of ornithology. The definitions come from aeronautics not from ornithology [and therein lies the revelation].[1]

—*Modelling the Flying Bird*

The Holy Thing That Got Me to This Moment

On the Hand That Has Held Me
All Along the Way

*P*rayers have been answered. And answered and answered. And, then, answered some more.

Which pretty much defines the beginning, middle, and end of this exercise in human devotion—in birthing and bonding and inevitably separating, though never completely, never every last cord to the heart—on this joyride called parenting. It surely explains what got us here to this holy moment: about to shuffle down a Jetway to board a plane to fly through the heavens to land at the doorstep of one college graduation.

The truest truth of parenthood, or at least the truest one for me, is that every stitch along this broadcloth of hope and faith and unwavering trust is one knotted with prayer.

From the instant someone back in that long-ago delivery room handed me that slippery, squirmy, wide-eyed babe, and then, not long after, pointed us toward the door to the big, wide, scary world beyond the hospital, I gulped and did the surest thing I could think of: I called on superpowers. Of the highest elevations. I let rip a mighty prayer. Insisted that angels and saints, almighty God, and holy mother Mary in all her maternal glories swoop down and blanket us, point the everlasting way, whisper answers to my nine gamillion questions—straight into my heart, the preferred route. And dare not take a coffee break.

Because I knew there was no way I could make it all on my own.

If left to my own devices long, long ago—if I'd not had that lifeline of prayer, and the knowledge that in my darkest hours, in the hours when I had no answers, and barely a trace of faith in anything worldly, there was a great and tender palm of a hand (honestly, I'd put in for a whole *flock* of palms of hands) cradling me and my growing-up child—I'd still be cowering behind that hospital door. I might still be crumpled at the knees wondering how we'd make it out alive.

To parent—to take a fresh-from-the-womb floppy creation and teach him or her the few things you know, and the volumes you cram in along the way—is to stare down every imaginable detour and distraction, to slay the thousand dragons that taunt you in innumerable forms: the playground bully, the out-of-control coach, and the rule that will not bend, to name but three. (I suppose I shouldn't forget my host of self-doubts and insecurities as perhaps the biggest dragons in the bunch.)

You see, I wouldn't know how to do that—how to let the air out of ugliness, how to crack at the knees those monsters who romp in the night—without my blessed backup squad: the angels and saints, the umpteen vigil lights and infinite vespers that are my hotline, my speed-dial, to God and assembled heavenly hosts.

One of the first things I learned when my kid went off to college—a steep climb of a first semester for me, not so for him—was that more than anything we'd stepped into the landscape of prayer. Especially when your kid is a thousand miles from home, and even you—hold-on-tight you—wouldn't dream of calling him, oh, every hour on the quarter hour.

I turned quickly to prayer. Prayer was, is, and ever will be my safety net.

I can't count the number of mornings I launched into daylight with prayers murmured before I flung back the sheets. I can't tally the times I turned toward the east-northeast to pinpoint my prayers somewhere in the vicinity of the appropriate dot on the compass, then let fly some litany of invocations, begging the heavens to be kind, to be gentle, to my faraway child.

As much as I prayed through the close-to-home years, I'd say I doubled the volume and depth in the long-distance years, the ones that in these modern times are more than likely to be our geographic realities.

The further you get into motherhood, the less likely your kid will put up with what might be your preferred proximity—tagging along right close to his side. So, once the squirt up and grows, you're left with a mama's number-one stand-in: the imperceptible prayers loosed from your heart and your tongue to the heavens above and beyond.

In the last four years, since that tear-sodden day when we dropped him alone on a green in the Land of Emily Dickinson, it's what's gotten the boy I love—or, certainly, his mama—through eight rounds of final exams, umpteen close calls, countless hours rowing the icy Connecticut River, one short trip across the Atlantic pond, a few emergency room visits, and a few late-night phone calls that stretched thinly—desperately—into the dawn.

As we step into the magical whirl of this weekend, when honors will be awarded and diplomas tucked in his once-little hand, as I stand back and marvel at this child who's now a deeply fine man, as I dab away rivers of tears and a heart that's frankly astounded, my every breath will be drawn in with a prayer, and let out with another.

I wouldn't be here, and neither would he, I am certain, if not for the Great Hand of the glorious and good God who reaches down and guides us each and every step of the way.

For this, I drop to my knees, in undying devotion for the one thing that got me to here: my deepest prayers answered.

Something of a postscript…

He Gave Us a Year: This Mama Will Never Forget

On Holy Hours, Gift Beyond Measure

The first inkling came a year ago December. It was a bitterly cold Sunday, and the voice on the line was one that had been making my heart skip since the first time I heard it. The words that followed were these: "Mommo, I've been thinking. I want to do something meaningful in the year between college and law school, and I can't think of anything more meaningful than being there for Tedd. I think I'll come home for a year."

Such is the sound of wishes come true. Of prayer you hadn't even put to words, come tumbling true. A mama's wildest hope.

So, on a sultry June afternoon, the old black sedan pulled down the alley. Out spilled my firstborn and a thousand-some boxes. A childhood bedroom was duly reordered. Carpet was ditched; floorboards, exposed. Old books, the books of a boyhood, were pulled and tossed in a box. College tomes took their place. Jobs were procured, the ones that would keep him busy by day. By night, he made his place at the side of the much younger brother, the brother just finding his way into high school, a high school with corridors known to be steep.

For one whole year, a year now gliding toward its close, big brother and little have entwined their hearts a little bit closer. There've been late-night runs for grilled cheese. And sartorial counsel proffered at the bathroom door. There've been soccer goals saved in front of the cheering—and very proud—older brother. And shoulder-to-shoulder talks on the couch, in the car, on the all-night airplane ride.

It was into his big brother's arms that the little one fell the morning our old cat died. The two of them crying, together. One of them wailing, "He was our third brother." Both of them wholly understanding the depth of that truth.

He was here for his brother, yes, but he was here, too, for the whole of us—night after night, as we sat, held hands, and whispered a prayer before picking up forks. Not one single dinner for four did I ever take for granted. Each one felt sacred. Felt numbered.

He was here in this unforgettable year, this year of loss as much as gain. He was here the day we got word that his grandpa had died; that very night, he stood by the side of his papa, both wrapped in their prayer shawls, at synagogue, on the eve of the most solemn Day of Atonement. He was there to hold his father's elbow during the Hebrew prayer of mourning. He was there to notice the tear that spilled from his father's eye. I was too. I saw and felt with my whole soul the presence of father and son standing shoulder to shoulder, prayer shawl to prayer shawl, in the hour of that father's deepest grief.

He was here, too, when friend after friend said goodbye before dying, in this year of hard loss. He was here to wrap his arm, and his laughter, around the grieving widower who has spent most every weekend with all of us, sopping up the pieces of his deeply shattered heart.

He was here for me, his old mama. The one who will never tire of long talks at the side of his bed, or chopping in sync at the kitchen counter. I never even minded the piles of laundry, knowing with each pair of boxers I folded that it was a task that wouldn't last. I considered it something akin to charming to iron old shirts, to track down orphaned socks.

The what's-next isn't quite worked out. But the calls are out. The interviews, scheduled. A move will be in the mix. I know that. I've always known that.

Which is what made this year the most priceless gift I could have imagined. A mother's gift beyond measure.

It was all a blessing. All wholly unexpected. All counter to cultural norms that these days send kids sailing post-college. He came home. He didn't mind—not so much, anyway—the questions from neighbors, the ones who might have looked askance at a kid whose only post-college option appeared to be a return to the roost. We knew otherwise. We knew the whole time.

He'd come home for one reason only: love.

He'd come home for the rare and breathtaking gift of stitching together two hearts. Hearts born eight years apart. Hearts whose plots on the lifeline had necessarily thrown them into parallel orbits—when one was learning to drive, the other was learning to read. When one was finding his way through a college quad, the other was starting middle school. But this year—one entering high school, one a man of the world and not too old to remember well the poignant trials of this particular high school— there was much deepening to be done. They could laugh at each other's jokes. Play each other's silly screen games. Bolster each other's hearts when either one was pummeled.

What they grew, over the shifting of seasons, over late nights and not-so-early mornings, was a brotherly love to last a lifetime.

I often flash forward in my mind's eye, imagine them calling each other in the long years ahead. I imagine their faces, lined with deepening grooves, the ones that come from living. I imagine their manly voices, calling long-distance—just to laugh, simply to celebrate, to be the front line in each other's rescue squad.

I once feared that the older one—long the only one—would be all alone after we'd gone. I know now, I pray now, that they'll long have each other's company—shared stories, shared love, unbreakable bond.

And so, on the brink of that second Sunday in May that honors motherhood, I find myself sated. I need no toast points ferried to bed. No violets clumped in a vase. I don't even need a hand-drawn card. I've lived and breathed a year I never expected. In the short story of my life, there will always be this one radiant whirl around the sun.

That's more than I'd ever have dreamed when someone once showed me the flickering spot on the ultrasound, the one they said was his heart, very much alive. The one that ever since has quickened the pulse of my own. My very own metronome, come home, all in the name of pure love.

From the Prayer Files . . .

A morning's benediction, to set us on our way, each and any day.

How Do the Heavens Know?

I can't begin to count the number of days it happens.

As the night lifts, as the dawn spreads across the landscape, as I begin to make out the shifting silhouettes of the grasses, of boughs, as a sparrow here, a cardinal there, begin to animate the tableau, I sense the day beginning to blanket me, soothe me, wrap my cold shoulders in what amounts to a shawl. A prayer shawl, more often than not.

So it was, when I awoke this day to a dawn draped in white. Snow on the bricks and the sharp blades of grass, just starting to stick. Snow on the bough beginning to clump. The world just beyond my windowpane, a filigree of shadow and palest of light.

How did the heavens know? How did the Great Beyond know that I needed a morning's blanket?

I needed stillness to step into.

The night had been long, had been tumbled. It was one of those nights when worry stitches each one of your dreams. You awake, yes, but you wonder if you've slept even a wink.

All you need on a morning like that is softness. Is quiet. You need a world on its tiptoes, padded tiptoes. You need a morning that, like an old friend, understands without words. Sidles up beside you, lays its head on your shoulder. Breathes.

The morning needn't rattle you. Needn't startle.

The morning comes softly. Snow tumbles down in flakes that shift from fat to fatter. You breathe. You inhale blessing, breath after breath, and then you let loose, your morning's litany, petition spiraling atop petition.

Dear God, watch over him. Dear God, protect her. Dear God, forgive us; forgive us our endless offenses, our trespasses, too. Dear God, forgive this globe that seems to be spinning too close to the edge of madness.

Dear God, fill us with grace. Give us strength. Give us wisdom. And, please, for once, let words fall from our lips with half the sense we'd hoped they would hold.

Dear God, blanket us. Open our eyes and our hearts. Show us the way. Let us startle someone in these hours ahead with some blast of unheralded goodness. Let us be the instrument of your peace. Let us pass over temptation, not be the one to whisper the word that would cut to the quick. Not turn the cold shoulder.

Dear God, steady us. Deepen us. Let me be the vessel this day that carries you into the midst of the chaos. Let me sow love. Let me bring pardon. Let me, in these hours ahead, scatter faith wherever there's doubt; hope, in place of despair.

You've answered my prayer before I've opened my eyes for the day. You've laced the dawn in white upon white, you've hushed the world out my window. You've opened my door into prayer—still heart, deep vow, bold promise.

Dear God, I thank you. Now let us tiptoe softly into this day.

Afterword: Aloft

Flight-bound: Navigating by stars, magnetic fields, or polarized light, with no guidance other than some inherited instinct, almost all first-year young will migrate without their parents—some of them hemisphere-to-hemisphere distances. The miles flown by a small but long-lived Arctic Tern can be equal to three trips to the moon and back. Half-ounce Blackpoll Warblers catch the trade winds far out in the Atlantic and fly south for 2,000 miles without rest, food, or water.[1]

—*Nests: Fifty Nests and the Birds that Built Them*

Winged Migration: Even the darkness moves with the passage of birds. On soft spring midnights, the air is alive with the flight notes of unseen warblers and vireos, thrushes and orioles, sparrows and tanagers, filtering through the moonlight like the voices of stars. Bird migration is the one truly unifying natural phenomenon in the world, stitching the continents together in a way that even great weather systems, which roar out from the poles but fizzle at the equator, fail to do. It is an enormously complex subject, perhaps the most compelling in natural history. That such delicate creatures undertake these epic journeys defies belief.[2]

—*Living on the Wind: Across the Hemisphere with Migratory Birds*

Afterword

And so our children someday soar. That's the hope, therein lies the heart of motherprayer. As our young take flight, we cast our eyes toward heaven's dome, tracing a trajectory—*their* trajectory—beyond our reach, perhaps, but never, ever, beyond our hearts.

Blessed be the winds that gyre and eddy beneath their wings, and the holy breath that enwraps us, carries us, infuses us, on this epic flight that is mothering. May our motherheart ever pulse with prayer. And may our pole-star be love beyond measure, far beyond the journey's end. Amen.

Acknowledgments

These pages might well be the living, breathing definition of "labor of love." More than anything these are love letters to my boys—that they might always hold in their hands, see before their eyes, a record of how deeply, intricately, and breathtakingly they were loved. That there might come a day when they're stirred to riffle through pages and sentences and particular choices of words to understand more deeply the love, the questions, the quandaries, the prayer they sparked in one mama's heart.

More than anyone, Will, my firstborn, and Teddy, my "little one," are the pulse points of these pages, the blessed muses who inspired every word. Writing their stories—capturing their words, their antics, the precise way they tumbled out of bed or down the stairs or plopped against the kitchen table—made me fall in love with them all over again, each time I sat down to type. With my whole heart, I thank them for putting up with a mama who's been known to scribble words they've spoken onto scraps of paper (within seconds of having spoken them), so just the way something was unspooled wouldn't be lost. I have tried mightily to preserve their dignity and the chambers dearest to their hearts and mine. I've extracted lessons that, I hope and pray, hold questions and truths whose weight extends far beyond the walls of our old shingled house. In fumbling for answers, I hope I've exposed only my own fault lines and not those of my most precious treasures.

If each book is gestational exercise, this one was safely in the hands and heart of Susan Salley, that rarest of editors in all the richest ways, and Roger Freet of Foundry Literary + Media, who shepherded an insistent idea to the delivery room door. And thus begins my emphatic litany of gratitude for all

Acknowledgments

who leapt into the birthing of this book: to the entire team at Abingdon Press, who shone on me the gift of their faith in my particular way of seeing the sacred in the ordinary messiness of the everyday. To Dawn Woods, kindred spirit, gentle heart from the start, for her vision both sweeping and fine-tuned. To Bruce DeRoos, blessed soul, who magically peered into my heart to pull out a cover wholly enchanting. To Susan Cornell, who saved me from grammatical, punctuational, and stylistic sins, meticulously shepherding these pages to the printing press, and becoming a friend along the way. To Nancy Watkins, my lasting treasure from my newspaper days, who in the sweetest reunion brought her editing pen and her unfailing writerly touch to each and every word on these pages. To Kelly Hughes, indispensable in every way—and a great and glorious soul, besides.

In the biology department, to Paul Ehrlich, David Dobkin, and Darryl Wheye, whose kindness and generosity allowed for the inclusion of avian field notes that so kindle my sense of wonder. And I would be stranded on a limb if not for the brilliant Laura Erickson, whose knowledge of birds is encyclopedic, exceeded only by the size of her heart.

To the motherfriends who have braved the course with me, bolstered me when I nearly buckled, wiped away my tears, taken my crazed phone calls, steadied me, and sent me on my way, chuckling all the while. Especially to my beloved Cecilia Vaisman, gone too soon, but not before lavishing hours of her attention on the questions of how in the world we might navigate the tightest motherly passages. To every brokenhearted friend who has ached to be a mother; to every mother who has borne the grief of burying a child, and too, the griefs that come in countless other guises. To the masterful mothers I've watched closely—studied, quite honestly—who've taught me, across the years, the most essential lessons in how to love wisely and with all my heart.

To my teachers in the trenches of daily journalism—beginning with John Teets, Nancy Watkins (again), Charles Leroux, Ann Marie Lipinski, Blair Kamin, Louise Kiernan. Ever, to Mark Burrows, poet and once-upon-a-landlord, who launched me on this book-lined road.

To my own mother, Mary Barbara, who for nearly twenty-four years has devoted her Tuesdays, and half as many Thursdays, to keeping my house afloat—and tummies filled—so I could type and type. To my long-gone papa, who sparked a lifelong love affair with words and history of the most personal matter. To my brother David, especially, and Becca Neumann, my sister by heart, traveling companions both, who share the intricacies of this odyssey, now near the beginning of their own. To Milo and Ella, because budding writers and artists should see in print how much they matter. To my mother-in-law, Ginny, who has never stopped believing that this book needed to be born.

To my sacred circle of Chair Sisters, without whom I'd have long ago crumpled up and skittered away.

From the bottom of my heart, to my one and only Blair, who insists on boldly and beautifully leaving a trail of words and, even more so, fine-chiseled ideas. And whose lessons in tenderness and patience were ones I've needed to learn, over and over.

And, from the beginning until beyond the end, to my holy blessed God, who holds me gently and fiercely and will not let me go. My most fervent prayer: may I ever be your pencil.

Notes

Epigraph

1. Rainer Maria Rilke, *Letters to a Young Poet*, trans. Stephen Mitchell (New York: Vintage, 1986), 34–35.

The Cradle That Is Prayer

1. Robert K. Barnhart, ed., *The Barnhart Dictionary of Etymology* (New York: H. W. Wilson, 1988), s.v. "cradle," 230; Douglas Harper, *Online Etymology Dictionary*, 2001, s.v. "cradle," http://etymonline.com/ (accessed September 18, 2014).

2. Anthony Grafton, "The Commonplace Bee: A Celebration," in *The Revolt of the Bees: Wherein the Future of the Paper-Hive Is Declared*, ed. Aaron Levy and Thaddeus Squire (Philadelphia: Slought Foundation, 2005), 35.

3. Harvard University Library Open Collections Program, "Commonplace Books," Reading: Harvard Views of Readers, Readership, and Reading History, http://ocp.hul.harvard.edu/reading/commonplace.html (accessed March 19, 2015).

4. While this is often the translation attributed to Saint Francis, the reference is rooted in chapter 17 of the First Rule of the Friars Minor issued in 1221, where the precise language, according to a 1905 translation by Father Paschal Robinson of *The Writings of Saint Francis of Assisi*, reads: "Let all the brothers preach by their works." Saint Francis of Assisi, *The Writings of Saint Francis of Assisi*, trans. Father Paschal Robinson (Philadelphia: Dolphin, 1905), 50.

On Field Notes

1. Robert G. Burgess, ed., *Field Research: A Sourcebook and Field Manual* (London: Routledge, 1989), 191–94.

2. Michael R. Canfield, ed., *Field Notes on Science & Nature* (Cambridge, MA: Harvard University Press, 2011), 16.

Nest Building

1. Paul R. Ehrlich, David S. Dobkin, and Darryl Wheye, *The Birder's Handbook: A Field Guide to the Natural History of North American Birds* (New York: Simon & Schuster, 1988), 369–71.

2. Ehrlich et al., 547.

3. Peggy Macnamara, *Architecture by Birds and Insects: A Natural Art* (Chicago: University of Chicago Press, 2008), 8.

4. Macnamara, xxi.

5. Julia Ward Howe, "Appeal to Womanhood Throughout the World," in *The Voice of Peace*, vol. 1, no. 6 (September 1874): 93.

6. F. Marian McNeill, *The Scots Kitchen: Its Traditions and Recipes* (Edinburgh: Birlinn, 2015). I cannot enthuse emphatically enough about this 1929 treasure, recently resurrected. I read it for its poetry as much as its recipes, evidenced in this one instruction from F. Marian, who advises that oats should be sprinkled over boiling water, "in a steady rain from the left hand and stirring it briskly the while with the right, sunwise."

7. Nigel Slater, "Nigel Slater's Classic Porridge Recipe," *The Guardian* online, www.theguardian.com/lifeandstyle/2011/jan/02/nigel-slater-classic -porridge-recipe (accessed January 13, 2016).

8. Felicity Cloake, "How to Cook Perfect Porridge," *The Guardian* online, www.theguardian.com/lifeandstyle/wordofmouth/2011/nov/10/how-to-cook -perfect-porridge (accessed January 13, 2016).

Mourning

1. Laura Erickson, "Western Scrub-Jay Funerals," *Laura Erickson's For the Birds* (blog), January 19, 2015, http://blog.lauraerickson.com/2015/01 /western-scrub-jay-funerals.html/ (accessed February 11, 2016). For years, Laura, author of a veritable flock of bird books, has been my go-to ornithology genius. We exchanged a flurry of e-mails about mama birds and mourning on February 11 and 12, 2016.

Hatchling

1. *Oxford English Dictionary*, 2nd ed., vol. 7, s.v. "hatchling"; *New Oxford American Dictionary*, 3rd ed., s.v. "hatchling."

2. Tim Birkhead, *The Most Perfect Thing: Inside (and Outside) a Bird's Egg* (New York: Bloomsbury USA, 2016), 44.

3. Ehrlich et al., 235.

4. Mark Bittman, *How to Cook Everything: Simple Recipes for Great Food* (New York: Macmillan, 1998), 662.

Brooding

1. Ehrlich et al., 61.
2. Charles G. Herbermann, ed., *The Catholic Encyclopedia*, vol. 13, s.v. "Sacraments" (New York: Robert Appleton, 1912), 297.

Tending the Clutch

1. Laura Erickson (producer, "For the Birds" podcast, former science editor Cornell Lab of Ornithology), e-mail exchange with the author, October 6, 2016.

Nestling

1. Barnhart, *Dictionary of Etymology*, s.v. "nestling," 701; Harper, *Online Etymology Dictionary*, s.v. "nestling," http://etymonline.com/ (accessed February 10, 2016).
2. "'Orphaned' Baby Birds," *All About Birds* (blog), Cornell Lab of Ornithology, www.birds.cornell.edu/AllAboutBirds/attracting/challenges/orphaned /document_view (accessed February 10, 2016).
3. Gertrud Mueller Nelson, *To Dance with God: Family Ritual and Community Celebration* (Mahwah, NJ: Paulist, 1986), 62.
4. Gavin Pretor-Pinney, *The Cloud Collector's Handbook* (San Francisco: Chronicle, 2011), 10.
5. Julee Rosso and Sheila Lukins, *The Silver Palate Cookbook* (New York: Workman, 1982), 276–77.

Fledgling

1. Barnhart, *Dictionary of Etymology*, s.v. "fledgling," 390; Harper, *Online Etymology Dictionary*, s.v. "fledgling" and "fledge," http://etymonline.com/ (accessed February 10, 2016).
2. "'Orphaned' Baby Birds," *All About Birds* (blog), Cornell Lab of Ornithology, www.birds.cornell.edu/AllAboutBirds/attracting/challenges/orphaned /document_view (accessed February 10, 2016).
3. Barbara Mahany, "Welcome Home, College Freshman. XOXO," *Chicago Tribune* (Nov. 20, 2011): Section 1, 23.

Notes

Almost Empty Nest

1. Ehrlich et al., 307.

2. Peg Bracken, *The I Hate to Cook Book* (New York: Harcourt, Brace & World, 1960), 8–9.

And in the End

1. C. J. Pennycuik, *Modelling the Flying Bird* (Amsterdam: Academic, 2008), 37–40.

Afterword

1. Sharon Beals, *Nests: Fifty Nests and the Birds that Built Them* (San Francisco: Chronicle, 2011), 11.

2. Scott Weidensaul, *Living on the Wind: Across the Hemisphere with Migratory Birds* (New York: North Point, 1999), x.